WITNESS: The Art of JE

www.nrm.org

WITNESS: The Art of JERRY PINKNEY

NORMAN ROCKWELL MUSEUM

WITNESS: The Art of

JERRY PINKNEY

Acknowledgments 6

Introduction: Witness: The Art of Jerry Pinkney 8
by Stephanie Haboush Plunkett

Call and Response 24
by Jerry Pinkney

Dream Catcher: Jerry Pinkney and the American Picturebook Tradition 34
by Leonard S. Marcus

American Illustrator 42
by Gerald L. Early, Ph.D.

Draw What You Know 52
by Steven Heller

Watercolor into Wood 60
by Joyce K. Schiller, Ph.D.

Catalogue Contributors 80

Exhibition Checklist 83

Acknowledgments

His Family Helped Him Build the Ark, 2002, Illustration for *Noah's Ark*

Dedicated to the art of illustration in all its variety, Norman Rockwell Museum is honored to present *Witness: The Art of Jerry Pinkney*, a retrospective exhibition tracing the fifty year journey of one of the most highly acclaimed children's book artists of our time.

Like millions of readers throughout the world, I have long admired Jerry Pinkney's elegant drawings, luminous watercolors, and beautifully conceived narratives, and have had the pleasure of inviting his participation in three previous installations. *The Art of Enchantment: Classic Tales by Contemporary Illustrators* (1995) was my first curatorial venture at the Norman Rockwell Museum, and Jerry's number was the first that I called. His illustrations for *The Last Tales of Uncle Remus* were exhibition highlights, clear signifiers of the installation's quality overall. *Pushing the Envelope: The Art of the Postage Stamp* (2000) and *National Geographic: The Art of Exploration* (2006) followed, and at each turn, his kind enthusiasm was evident, and deeply appreciated by our staff and the many visitors to our galleries. These group exhibitions revealed distinct aspects of this versatile artist's work, and we are thrilled now to shed light on the richness of his creativity through each phase of his illustrious career.

Our sincere thanks to Jerry Pinkney for his support in making this important exhibition possible at the Norman Rockwell Museum, and to Gloria Jean Pinkney, for her inspiration throughout the planning process. *Witness: The Art of Jerry Pinkney* is made possible, in part, with generous support from The Max and Victoria Dreyfuss Foundation, and from, Penguin Group, Inc., and Little, Brown Books for Young Readers, A Division of The Hachette Group—venerable publishers, who have worked in partnership with Jerry Pinkney for many years. Their assistance is greatly appreciated, with special thanks to Lauri Hornik and Marirosa Mia Garcia of Penguin Group, Inc., and Andrea Spooner and Victoria Stapleton of Little, Brown Books for Young Readers, Hachette Book Group USA. Mimi Kayden's kind willingness to part with treasured collections has also helped to ensure a stellar installation.

We are grateful to essayists Dr. Gerald L. Early, Steven Heller, Leonard S. Marcus, and our gifted exhibition co-curator Dr. Joyce K. Schiller for their insightful contextual commentary, which provides important new scholarship relating to the artist's work. Thanks also to Rita Marshall for her exquisite catalogue design, with assistance from Mindy Belter, and to Chuck Gillett, Suzanne Salinetti and their talented team at The Studley Press, Inc. in Dalton, Massachusetts, for their outstanding work on this publication. The valiant efforts of Norman Rockwell Museum Exhibitions Manager Russell Horton, Manager of Collections and Registration Martin Mahoney, Manager of Traveling Exhibitions Mary Melius, Curator of Archival Collections Corry Kanzenberg, Marketing Director Margit Hotchkiss, Meida Services Manager Jeremy Clowe, and Webmaster Dan Heck are deeply appreciated, as is the support of Director/CEO Laurie Norton Moffatt, who joins me in celebrating the power of illustrated images in our world.

Stephanie Haboush Plunkett
Deputy Director / Chief Curator
Norman Rockwell Museum

WITNESS:
The Art of Jerry Pinkney

Stephanie Haboush Plunkett

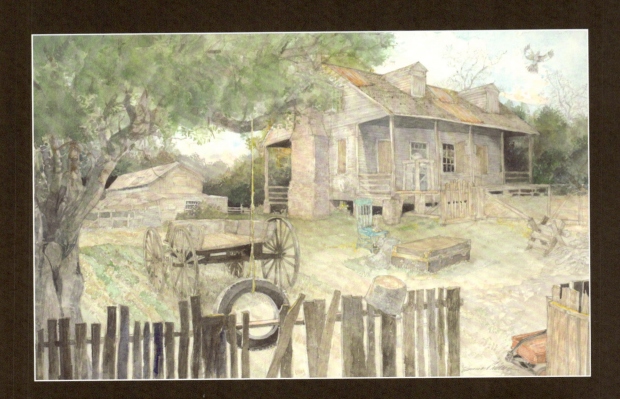

"**I'VE** found it interesting to trace how the chapters of my life have knitted themselves into my art." — *Jerry Pinkney*

In its purest sense, the act of artistic creation is a bit like looking at oneself in the mirror and leaving one's reflection behind. All that an artist is, all that he believes, and the many things that he has witnessed in his time, become one with his art.

Across his fifty year journey as an illustrator, Jerry Pinkney has cast a warm, curious eye on our world to create transcendent images that reflect his passion for life, his love of family and community, and his deep and abiding engagement with the rich complexities of history. A master watercolorist with a distinct personal message to convey, he reminds us that no act of kindness, however small, is ever wasted, in elegant images that celebrate life's small but extraordinary moments, the wonders of classic literature, and the wisdom of those who have gone before us.

Born of a life-long desire to connect with others through art, Pinkney's heartfelt icons of living culture have, since 1960, been a part of the American visual landscape in ways that are integral to our lives. Initially created for the covers and pages of periodicals and picture books, postage stamps, greeting cards, product advertisements, and well-traveled historic sites rather than for the walls of galleries and museums, his art is intimately encountered by a vast and eager audience seeking meaning and enrichment in the stories that he tells. In his illustrations, intricately conceived narratives imbue ordinary activities with a sense of historical importance, and exquisite characters and details inspire belief by millions in the vision that he continues to refine.

Born on December 22, 1939, and raised in the Germantown section of Philadelphia, an ethnically diverse neighborhood in which African Americans built community among themselves, Pinkney never imagined that a career in art might be possible. In his modest but loving home, he was the middle born in a family of six children, and was recognized for his creativity at a young age. Encouraged by his mother Willie Mae, a homemaker, and his father James, a craftsman with a flair for style who specialized in decorative wall papers and painting for a regional clientele, Pinkney took full advantage of the wood, building supplies, and paints in his father's workshop, imagining a world apart from the day to day. Some of the artist's earliest sketches were made on the backs of wall paper samples, his father's tool in trade. "I was drawing to learn," Pinkney later reflected, "but no one was able to point me to a way of making a living in art."

Though visits to museums and galleries were not a part of life as a child, storytelling was treasured oral tradition at home. Pinkney's parents, who migrated from the South, read and

retold classic folk tales in rhythmic cadences that captured his imagination, providing a sense of cultural belonging. The legend of John Henry, *Uncle Remus* adventures of Brer Rabbit and his cohorts, and the classic story of *The Ugly Duckling*, all illustrated by the artist later in life, were among his favorites. Helen Bannerman's *The Story of Little Black Sambo* was treasured among the books in his family's library, despite its critical reevaluation. "The story of a small boy of color who exhibited courage and wit, and triumphed over something much larger than himself," was both appealing and affirming for him.

Life in the city provided a tapestry of visual interest for the young artist, who sketched shop window displays and observed passers-by between sales at the newspaper stand where he worked. Among his customers was cartoonist John J. Liney (1912–1982), a native Philadelphian best-known for his forty-four year post as artist for the daily syndicated comic strip, *Henry*, created by Carl Thomas Anderson in 1933. Impressed with Pinkney's work, Liney invited him for a studio visit, which offered him a first glimpse into the professional world of published art.

At Dobbins Vocational High School in Philadelphia, Pinkney immersed himself in the commercial art program, taking courses in calligraphy, drafting, and graphic design. He made time to draw from the live model in the evenings, excelling in his classes. Gloria Jean Pinkney, the artist's wife and then fellow Dobbins student, fondly recalls the intensity with which he went about his work, "with his sleeves rolled up and…a pencil behind his ear."

Photograph by Booker Fulmore, n.d., Jerry Pinkney's childhood home on Earlham Street in Philadelphia
Photographer Unknown, 1957, Jerry Pinkney's High School Graduation Picture

Despite his efforts and positive reviews from Dobbins teachers, Pinkney and other African American students were discouraged from applying for available art school scholarships because it was unlikely that they could forge professional careers in the field. Determined to succeed, Pinkney obtained applications for himself and others, and along with a close friend, was accepted at the Philadelphia School of Art in 1957 as a design student and a scholarship recipient.

The art school experience was rich for Pinkney, and it enhanced his awareness of opportunities in the visual arts. "Once the illustration department gave the design department an illustration project to work on," he recalled. "Our work was fresh and indicative of what was going on in the commercial art field at the time. After that, I found myself solving design problems through drawing." A designer with an emerging interest in the art of illustration, Pinkney took his first professional step in 1960, at The Rust Craft Greeting Card Company in Dedham, Massachusetts, the second largest publisher of greeting cards in the nation at the time. Before being hired, he prepared a portfolio of drawings appropriate for the company's line, and realized then that illustration was the path he wished to pursue.

At the time, Boston had an active publishing industry that nurtured emerging artists. In the years that followed, Pinkney further explored the art of illustration at Barker-Black Studio, where he created imagery for advertising, annual reports, and text books. At Barker-Black, he produced his first illustrated picturebook, *The Adventures of Spider: West African Folk Tales* by Joyce Cooper Arkhurst, published in 1964. The artist's playful, stylized drawings traced the antics of the West African trickster and reflected his love of design, storytelling, and the language of line—the first of many artworks for picture books to come. While in Boston, he co-founded Kaleidoscope, an independent art studio serving a diverse client base, and deepened his commitment to illustration in 1965, when he made the bold decision to launch a career as a freelance artist.

Boston had much to recommend it for Pinkney. A sizeable but intimate city, it inspired growth and change through exposure to other talented creators, including those of color. "A sense of community has always been important to me," he said. "I understood very early that I could not evolve as an artist or as a person without being connected to institutions that served the community." He designed catalogues and posters for the Elma Lewis School of Fine Arts and the National Center for Afro-American Artists, and recalled the power of his first exposure to original artworks by Jacob Lawrence (1917-2000), Romare Bearden (1911-1988), Charles Wilbert White (1918-1979), Hale Woodruff (1900-1980), and Horace Pippin (1888-1946) in the exhibition *Five Black Artists*, which previewed there.

As his interests turned toward imagery and its relationship to literature, the wonders of narrative storytelling were also brought to life by encounters with the work of legendary illustrators. Original paintings for literary classics by N.C. Wyeth (1882-1945) captured his attention in a publisher's waiting room where they were on display, and he was "impressed by the scale of Wyeth's works and by what he expressed, the drama, the sense of place, and the narrative." Studying Wyeth's paintings up-close proved inspirational, and gifts of books like *The Wonder Clock* by Howard Pyle (1853-1911), and *Aesop's Fables* and *The Wind in the Willows*, both illustrated by Arthur Rackham (1867-1939), sparked his imagination, instilling in him a desire to create expressive pictures. "These books…spoke to the whole manner of creating art—the surface, the texture, and the richness—that I had not understood."

As he and Gloria Jean raised their young family, opportunities to illustrate picture books illuminating the folk tales and fairy tales of diverse cultures emerged, and the artist challenged himself to create true authenticity in his art. During the 1960s, the unwritten conventions of mid-century that avoided depictions of ethnicity in published art began to fall away, inspired by public demand for more inclusive cultural representations. As a father, and as an illustrator striving to avoid stereotype and convey cultural resonance, he began to understand art's power to construct perceptions about race and society. His empathetic depictions reflected his own compassionate nature, and his dream of being "a strong role model for my family and other African Americans" was becoming a reality.

By the time he moved west to the New York metropolitan area in 1970 seeking additional outlets for his art, he had already received high professional accolades and public recognition. Book publishers increasingly engaged his artistic abilities to illustrate stories inspired by the realities of the African American experience, like Mildred D. Taylor's 1975 *Song of the Trees*, a poignant reflection on the challenges of life during the Great Depression, and *Childtimes: A Three Generation Memoir* by Eloise Greenfield and Lessie Jones Little, published in 1975.

In addition, corporations offered high-profile commissions, carrying historical conscience more deeply into popular culture. A lover of music—from jazz and blues to classical—Pinkney has collected books on its visual interpretation for years, and enjoyed the chance to illustrate album covers for RCA Records and calendars honoring jazz greats of the Harlem Renaissance for The Smirnoff Company. Distributed widely by Seagram Distillers in the mid-1970s, Pinkney's

exquisite series of calendars and posters, illustrated in watercolor, look back on significant people and events in African American history, from the arrival of the first African slaves to the Great Migration and the Voting Rights Act of 1965. Originally among Seagrams' corporate art collections, the thirty-five original paintings in Pinkney's African American *Journey to Freedom* series are now preserved and interpreted by the Schomburg Center for Research in Black Culture in New York City.

In 1978, the United States Postal Service invited him to create the first of twelve postage stamps, including a series of Black Heritage portraits honoring the contributions of notable African American freedom fighters, statesmen, athletes, and musicians, the first nine in an ongoing series that places palm-sized pieces of history into millions of hands. On behalf of the Postmaster General, he served on the Citizen's Stamp Advisory Committee for ten years, from 1982 to

On the Ground Lay Countless Trees, 1975, Illustration for *Song of the Trees*

1992, charged with providing a breadth of judgment and depth of experience that influenced the subject matter, character, and beauty of American postage stamps.

Limited edition releases by The Franklin Library, then the nation's largest distributor of classic books designed for the collector's market, featured Pinkney's work in the late 1970s by aligning his art with texts by acknowledged literary giants. *Gulliver's Travels*, a full-length satirical work by Jonathan Swift charting the escapades of the fictional surgeon and ship captain Lemuel Gulliver; and *These Thirteen* by William Faulkner, the author's first mass release short story collection, were welcome projects. Despite struggles with dyslexia since childhood, the artist has always taken time to read manuscripts carefully, and credits his slower paced reading with an ability to absorb and portray details that might otherwise go unnoticed.

In the 1970s, Pinkney's art for contemporary works of historical fiction helped establish engagement with the experiences of people of color, particularly for middle grade readers. Book jackets for the Newbery Medal winner, *Roll of Thunder, Hear My Cry* by Mildred Taylor, a story of an African American family's Depression-era experiences, and *Steal Away: Stories of Runaway Slaves* by Abraham Chapman, among others, became the face of living, breathing characters who moved through their pages. These and other commissions, including a powerful and methodically researched series of artworks for *National Geographic*'s 1984 "Escape from Slavery: The Underground Railroad," were important visual documents for the artist. "I was trying to use these projects as vehicles to address the issues of being an African American, and the importance of African American contributions to society," he said. "I wanted to be a strong role model, and to show my children the possibilities that lay ahead for them. That was very important."

Family loomed large in important mid-career works that opened a window onto the everyday lives of African Americans. His illustrations for *The Patchwork Quilt*, Valerie Flournoy's poignant 1985 reflection on the intergenerational bonds within an African American family, were pivotal for the artist. The book's appearance on PBS television's Reading Rainbow, which promoted independent reading by featuring quality literature for children, brought its message to an appreciative audience and signified success. The 1990 book *Home Place* by Cresent Dragonwood re-imagines an abandoned rural home and the family who once lived there. Pinkney's warm, humanizing portrayals of people from the past, joyful views of nature, and interiors replete with floral wallpapers remembered from his childhood, establish a positive, empathetic view.

In the 1990s, *Back Home* and *The Sunday Outing*, two books written by Gloria Jean Pinkney

and illustrated by the artist, brought family memories and traditions to light. A captivating storyteller in the oral tradition, Gloria was encouraged to develop narratives for publication by her husband and family, who had always enjoyed the richness of her rememberings. "She had a great understanding of story structure having read so many of the manuscripts that came across my desk," Pinkney said, "and she had many interesting childhood stories to tell."

Another enduring collaboration between gifted creators was launched in 1987 when Pinkney was invited by his publisher to illustrate *The Tales of Uncle Remus*, retold by American author, educator, and musician Julius Lester. "Another artist was working with Julius initially but could not complete the project," he said. "In my youth, Uncle Remus tales were read and told to us," but as enthusiastic about the opportunity as he was, he also understood the book's controversial nature. "Working for the first time on stories that really had bruised people" was concerning for him, but he maintained the goal of capturing the spirit within each piece, leaving the stereotypical behind. Fascinated by wildlife, he established the anthropomorphic qualities of Brer Rabbit, Brer Bear, and many others by emphasizing their humanistic characteristics and portraying them in natural settings. The artist's reference library on nature and animals came in handy, as did a full length mirror in which he could act out his own interpretations of creature behavior.

Tanya Stopped at the Room Aunt Kay Had Called Her Sitting Parlor, 1995, Illustration for *Tanya's Reunion*

In addition to three other volumes continuing their popular series of Uncle Remus adaptations, Pinkney worked closely with Lester on other important works inspired by cultural narratives, including *John Henry*, a childhood favorite that offered the opportunity, in 1994, to "create an African American hero that would inspire all." Familiar, too, was the story of Ybo Landing that inspired Lester's masterpiece, *The Old African*—a stirring legend infused with magical realism that he and Pinkney brought to life more than five years later, in 2005.

"I remember vividly my first reading of *The Old African*, conscious of the possibility that it could be my next illustration project. I was stunned at the power and poetry of its creative language. But is seemed to me that Julius's masterful text was complete in itself," Pinkney said. "I couldn't help but ask myself, 'What role could I play'?" He visited the Schomburg Center for Research in Black Culture to immerse himself in information about the enslavement of the Ybo, and reached out to John Oriji, an African historian of Ybo origin. With research in place, he entered the story's time and space to inhabit each character, drawing and redrawing over and over again. Illustrations for *The Old African* took two years to complete—a labor of love in tribute those whose struggle is remembered.

Published in 1998, *Black Cowboy, Wild Horses: A True Story* brought Pinkney and Lester together to highlight the contributions of people of color on the frontier. An African American cowboy and a former slave, Bob Lemmons was known for his horsemanship and his gentle way with wild mustangs. The artist's dynamic, textural paintings provide sensory depictions of Lemmons' struggle and triumph over the unforgiving plains. "As a boy growing up in the 1940s, Westerns were huge. We all played cowboys, practicing our quick draw with toy holsters and guns," remembered the artist. "I found out later that many cowboys were black and Mexican, as were stagecoach drivers, saloon proprietors, laborers, and explorers." Pinkney's exquisite depictions of horses in

Brer Rabbit Scares Everybody, 1987, Illustration for *The Tales of Uncle Remus*

The Hoof Prints of Mustangs, 1998, Illustration for *Black Cowboy, Wild Horses*

There's Something I Want to Show You, 1996, Illustration for *Minty: A Story of a Young Harriet Tubman*

Amelia (c.1762) and *Cuffee* (1741), 2008, Illustrations for the African Burial Ground Interpretive Center, New York

every posture and gait came through careful observation, and their behavioral patterns were gleaned from the experts who willingly shared their knowledge.

In other books like *Minty: A Story of Young Harriet Tubman* by Alan Schroeder Pinkney uses the few known facts about historical figures to bring their stories to life, a skill he has brought to site specific commissions, of which he is rightfully proud. Among them, a series of powerful life-size figures gave presence to documented northern slaves at the African American Burial Ground Interpretive Center in New York, in 2008. For the artist, the project unleashed the notion that slavery occurred only in the south. "My role was to individualize the people who were buried there, to give a face to history." He received brief descriptions of well and little-known figures,

Freedman's Village c. 1864, 2007, Brochure Illustration for Arlington House, The Robert E. Lee Memorial, Virginia all of whom were buried at the site. A slave named Mary is shown tending a garden outside of the city, carrying her eight-month-old son in a cloth sling on her back. Her only mention is found in a will from around 1707, and additional facts pertaining to the clothing that she wore are surmised from historical knowledge of her time. Portraits of Pinkney's subjects were not extant, so likenesses were inspired by those of others who came as slaves from similar regions in Africa.

"As I worked on these figures," Pinkney said, "I could not speak their names. Only after completing the art was I able to make the connection that they were real people, especially the child, who is without hope." Frail and work-worn, young Amelia (c.1762) was a particularly wrenching subject for the artist. Amelia's mother Belinda, whom he also portrayed, is seen with her well-fed charge rather than her own child.

Among several National Park Service projects was a series of site brochure illustrations documenting slavery at Arlington House, the home of Robert E. Lee and his family in Virginia. Pinkney visited the site and researched the lives, responsibilities, and treatment of Arlington House slaves, establishing recreations based in fact. His artworks, published in 2007, provide a visual record that is essential to historical understanding, made possible only by the heart, mind and hand of the artist. Other site experiences that have been enhanced by his imagery include the Booker T. Washington National Historic Site in Virginia and the George Washington Carver National Monument in Missouri.

"I am a storyteller at heart," Jerry Pinkney reminds us, even after a half century of imagemaking. "There is something special about knowing that your stories can alter the way people see the world, and their place within it." Always rooting for the underdog, he continues to make images that are bear witness to his underlying belief that all things are possible. Whether recreating history or breathing new life into classic tales, his art is always about much more than just the appearance of things. Reaching beyond their aesthetic and conceptual underpinnings, his illustrations reveal larger truths that offer invaluable insights into who we are, and who we might become.

House and Garden in India, 1997, Title Page Illustration for *Rikki-Tikki-Tavi*

CALL AND RESPONSE

Jerry Pinkney

THERE is a story that was told by my mother of when at a very early age I was often found tucked in a corner beneath the keyboard of our upright piano, making pictures. My sisters all state, "There was something different about Jerry." From as far back as I can remember I have had this overwhelming need to draw.

There was no artist in my family, among our friends, or in our neighborhood that I was aware of. I didn't meet a professional artist until my twelfth year, which was when the idea of practicing art saw the light of day and gained traction. Now, at the age of seventy, after fifty years of making images, it is a curious matter to trace those introductory steps that led to my being open, thirsty, and equipped to embrace this novel notion.

I grew up in the Germantown section of Philadelphia, Pennsylvania. Our home was a small two-story red brick row house on a dead-end street. Residing at 51 East Earlham were my mother Willie Mae, my father James H., three sisters, and two brothers. I was the youngest son and middle child. We all shared five rooms with a single bath which was without a sink.

My mother was a homemaker and occasional day worker. She was largely responsible for keeping her children well fed, clothed, and disciplined. Willie Mae loved to read. She read from the Bible and the writings of Ralph Waldo Emerson, and to her children she read the classic fairy and folk tales. I am dyslexic, and even with my challenges in reading, I understood, through her, the power of literature and how it can inform one's inner life.

My mother's reading chair was alongside our living room window, one of the few that let sunlight in. There on a table beside it, my mother grew tall houseplants. As a young boy I was fascinated by her small patch of a flower garden. It was an oasis in our urban setting. Those plants and their blossoms with sunlight filtering through became the inspiration and subject of an early painting in art school.

My father was a fiercely independent man who relished his job selling produce in a local grocery store. However, after some time, he left steady employment to become his own boss. He worked at radio and television repair, electrical work, plumbing, house painting, lawn care, and refinishing furniture. Dad would attempt to fix or paint anything. At one time, he had some leftover pink paint, and used it on our piano.

When I was young, he taught me ways to take old furniture and restore it by bringing the grain

Photograph of Jerry Pinkney by Myles Pinkney, c. 1990

of aged wood back to life. Dad's workshop was in the basement of our home. There I found the tools he worked with, including leftover wall paper, which I was given. Upon turning the patterns over, I proceeded to draw pictures. Oftentimes when Dad was off working, I would spend time in his cramped cluttered cellar, experiencing the feel of his tools. Most importantly, I loved the idea of making something and using my imagination to alter and change things. Dad's workshop was a fertile place that gave spark and flight to my creative spirit.

Both of my parents encouraged my interests and exploits. To this day I am not sure why this support was given. Neither parent went further than elementary school. They showed little curiosity about the visual arts. Our family never visited an art museum or gallery. I wonder if supporting my interests was simply a way for my parents to feed me something they saw as a positive thing for me to do in my spare time.

With family and friends having migrated from the South, it is perhaps no surprise that I became well acquainted with the oral tradition of storytelling. The stories that I so fondly remember, like *John Henry* and *The Tales of Uncle Remus*, were told to me as a boy.

Wood Wall, 2003, Illustration for *God Bless the Child*

I attended an all Black elementary school. After school and during the summer months, the children of Earlham Street had more than enough time to fill. It was not only where I lived, but where I played. There were no boys clubs or swimming pools available. Once you left our block the surrounding families were Italian and Jewish. There was little socializing with these families in my growing up years, though I did on occasion play with the children of my father's wealthy clients. The families of color on Earlham Street were my world. In 1952, I enrolled in Roosevelt Junior High School, which was integrated. Is it any wonder that the crossroads of the 1940s and 1950s fostered the need in me to create works intended to draw people together?

With an irresistible urge to make things, I spent hours at a time in my room drawing or out on the block with friends. It was a creative time. We invented games, whittled things out of wood, and built clubhouses out of found materials. Then there were those special days when we ventured to the local movie house. Captivated by cowboy movies, my buddies and I would attempt those narratives when we returned home by fashioning costumes out of things we made or purchased at the five-and-dime store. Earlham Street became our Wild West. We explored

Then the Rain Came, 1998, Illustration for *Black Cowboy, Wild Horses*
Following page: *Escape at Night*, 1996, Illustration for *The Underground Railroad Handbook*, National Park Service, 1997

the new frontier, rounded up cattle, and put bad guys in jail. We took turns being Roy Rogers, Gene Autry, and Daniel Boone. I even carved a bowie knife modeled after the one Jim Bowie wore on his side at the Alamo. In later life, I learned that one out of every three cowboys was either Black or Mexican, and that people of color were also a part of the exploration of the West. There were Black stagecoach drivers, sheriffs, mail carriers, and saloon proprietors.

About that same time, I discovered that a historical site was just a short distance from our home. The Johnson House was a prominent station on the Underground Railroad. Hundreds of escaping slaves were sheltered there on their way further North. How incredible it is to realize that I walked just a few blocks from it on my way to Hill Elementary School. Could growing up in a place so rich in the history of the anti-slavery movement have affected my future interests? Could my world of play have inspired the search for projects that tell the stories I hungered for as a child? It had to have been these early influences that strengthened and helped to shape my imagination and curiosity.

left: Photographer Unknown. James and Willie Mae Pinkney, c. 1940
right: Photographer Unknown. Jerry Pinkney (l) as a boy on Earlham Street with sister Joan, c. 1941

Everybody in our tiny house had to stake claim to private space. My mother had her reading chair with its island of plants and my father had his basement workshop. I'm not certain how my brothers and sisters found their personal spaces, but for me it was my small sketchbook.

When I was twelve, my first job was selling newspapers at the intersection of Germantown and Chelten Avenues. Every day, I would perch on a shelf of my newsstand and draw people and the display windows in a nearby department store, treating each new window display like a rotating still life.

John Liney (1912–1982), the Philadelphia cartoonist who drew the syndicated comic strip *Henry* for forty-four years, bought his newspaper from me daily. One day he took note of my sketching. He asked if I might share my drawings with him. I don't recall if he critiqued my work. However, Mr. Liney did extend an invitation for a visit to his nearby studio. My time with this generous person and witnessing his creative process is where I found my muse…art.

In this exhibition, one will find a body of work anchored in many early experiences and

left: Photographer Unknown. Jerry and Gloria Jean Maultsby at her high school prom, 1959
right: Photographer Unknown. Jerry and Gloria Jean Pinkney and young family, 1965

observations. There are other notable benchmarks in my journey. I began my studies in 1957 at the Philadelphia School of Art. In 1960, I married Gloria Jean Maultsby and we moved with our daughter to Boston, where I was employed by The Rust Craft Greeting Card Company of Dedham, Massachusetts. In 1963, I joined the staff at The Barker Black Design and Illustration Studio. Around 1965, along with three other artists, Rob Howard, George Price, and Joe Veno, we worked under the name Kaleidoscope Studio. In 1967, I became a freelance artist, working out of a fourth-floor studio in Boston's South End, where I lived with Gloria and our four children. Gloria played a large role in raising our children but also held a unique and valued place in my creative process as a researcher, office manager, and astute commentator on my art.

In Boston, I created two illustrations for an Allyn and Bacon series titled *This is Music*. These watercolors mark the beginning of *Witness: The Art of Jerry Pinkney*—significant stops along a steep learning arc from 51 Earlham Street to the Norman Rockwell Museum, an extraordinary journey that has lasted over fifty years. I am, to this day, just as committed and energized by those early callings to explore subjects, and to respond by making art.

Photograph by Myles Pinkney. Jerry Pinkney in his Croton-on-Hudson, New York Studio

DREAM CATCHER:
Jerry Pinkney and the American Picture-book Tradition

Leonard S. Marcus

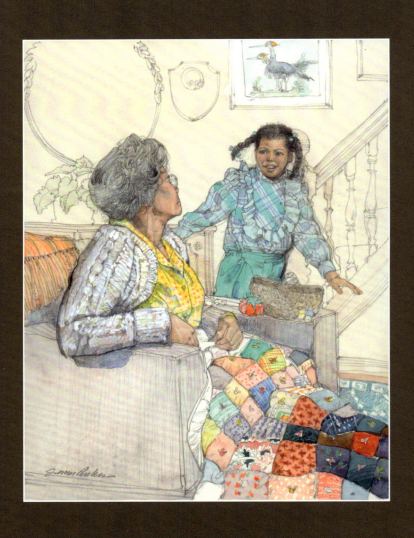

IN 1963, the American Library Association awarded the Randolph Caldecott Medal, its prestigious annual prize for the most distinguished work of illustration for children by an American, to Ezra Jack Keats for *The Snowy Day*, a picture book about the idyllic winter adventures of a young boy named Peter. A notable feature of the illustrations was the artist's decision (nowhere suggested by the text) to depict Peter as an African American. The last American picture books to feature a black child had appeared nearly two decades earlier. Keats, the Brooklyn-born son of Eastern European Jewish immigrants, had clearly meant to make a statement. So too, it seems fair to assume, had the committee of fifteen librarians who voted to confer the very public honor on the artist and his book.

The following year, Jerry Pinkney, on assignment as a staff artist with The Barker Black Design and Illustration studio, in Boston, illustrated a storybook for children called *The Adventures of Spider: West African Folk Tales*, with a text by Joyce Cooper Arkhurst. The client and publisher was the old Boston firm of Little, Brown. For Pinkney, who had trained for a career in advertising and editorial illustration, the project provided a refreshing excursion into the realm of books. Coming at a time of growing personal involvement in the civil rights movement and of a deepening identification with his African American heritage, the assignment also tied together important aspects of his life and work in a satisfying way. Still, as Pinkney later told an interviewer, "I did not yet see myself as an artist who might one day illustrate a contemporary story such as *The Patchwork Quilt* ... [or] feel that through such books [on African American subjects] I could make a contribution to society." (*WAYS*, 157-58)

As a father with young children at home, Pinkney knew *The Snowy Day* and understood that its publication was a landmark event. But he was also acutely aware of the dearth of picture books with contemporary African American themes. To skeptics the very success of Keats's book smacked of tokenism. Educator and critic Nancy Larrick said as much in *The Saturday Review of Literature*. In her essay "The All-White World of Children's Books" (September 11, 1965), Larrick issued a broad indictment of American publishing, taking industry executives to task not only for the whites-only focus of the books they published for young people but also their failure to attract editorial personnel of color. She noted one bright spot: the recent founding of the Council on Interracial Books for Children, a watchdog and advocacy group that in 1968 would go on to launch an award aimed at securing first-time publication for talented African American authors and illustrators. Larrick's jeremiad appeared just weeks after the Watts riots and within months of

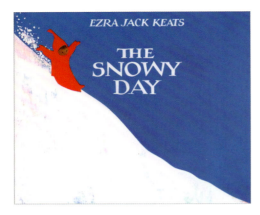

the assassination of Malcolm X, the nonviolent march from Selma to Birmingham, Alabama, led by Dr. Martin Luther King Jr., and the signing into law of the Voting Rights Act. It prompted a period of industry-wide soul-searching, and may be said to have helped prepare the ground for the publication of *Stevie* (1969), a picture book about a modern-day urban, single-parent childhood, written in black dialect, and featuring raw, expressionist illustrations reminiscent of Rouault. Such was the excitement surrounding the release of this unconventional book by John Steptoe, an African American artist still in his teens, that *Life* magazine profiled Steptoe and reprinted the story in full, and *The Today Show* invited him on for an interview—both rare accolades indeed for the author of a juvenile. The frenzied media response seemed in fact to reflect an uneasy mix of genuine appreciation and residual white guilt. Progress during the 1960s toward a more inclusive vision of American children's literature was nothing if not fitful nonetheless, the progress was real.

Two earlier efforts to publish books inspired by a similar vision had ended in disappointment. In 1920, in the hopeful afterglow of the armistice that brought an end to the First World War, W.E.B. Du Bois had thought the moment was right to plant seeds of racial pride in the younger generation by creating a monthly magazine for African American children that offered the finest examples of poetry, prose, art, and photography. *The Brownies' Book* had its origins in an annual special issue of the NAACP's major publication, *The Crisis*, and was intended to provide children of color with an acceptable alternative to mainstream juvenile magazines such as the much-touted *St. Nicholas*, which while upholding high aesthetic standards peppered its pages with casually offensive references to race. Langston Hughes had his first publication in *The Brownies' Book*. Harlem Renaissance novelist Nella Larsen also wrote for the magazine. The actor Charles S. Gilpin, star of the original cast production of Eugene O'Neill's *The Emperor Jones*, discussed his life as an actor. For all its editorial excellence, *The Brownies' Book* did not win the public support it needed to sustain itself. Du Bois's ambitious experiment on behalf of the "children of the sun" lasted all of two years.

Title page image for *The Snowy Day*, © 1962 by Ezra Jack Keats

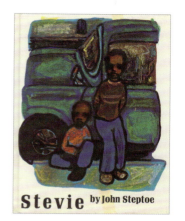
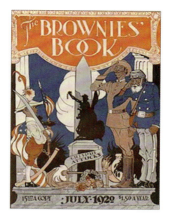

The Brownies' Book would today be considered an alternative press publication. In contrast to that "outsider" venture, the second major attempt at creating a children's literature about African American experience came from within the establishment, through the initiative of a few idealistic publishing figures of the 1930s and 1940s. Shortly before her retirement from Macmillan, pioneering editor Louise Seaman Bechtel published Langston Hughes and Arna Bontemps' *Popo and Fifina: Children of Haiti* (1932). At Harcourt, Brace, and later at William Morrow, Elisabeth Bevier Hamilton championed books that depicted African Americans past and present in a respectful light. *Two Is A Team*, one of several books Hamilton published by Lorraine and Jerrold Beim (illustrated by Ernest Crichlow, 1945), told the story of two young friends, one black the other white, who played together in a spirit of unselfconscious camaraderie. Two years later with *North Star Shining: A Pictorial History of the American Negro*, by Hildegarde Hoyt Swift, also illustrated by Ernest Critchlow (1947), Hamilton offered young readers a pantheon of African American heroes, both famous and obscure, to look up to and emulate. The absence of comparable books on later lists overseen by Hamilton suggests that the response to the books she had already published in this vein had been less than hoped for. Hamilton, too, had failed to move the mountain.

The depth of the resistance faced by Hamilton and others may be inferred from the rough treatment accorded to Ellen Tarry, a black writer from Harlem, who had been recruited to write stories of young children of color by the Bank Street College of Education's visionary founder Lucy Sprague Mitchell. As a member of the Bank Street Writers' Laboratory, Tarry produced a

left: Cover image for *Stevie*, © 1969 by John L. Steptoe
right: Cover image for *The Brownies' Book*, © 1920 by W. E. B. Du Bois

picture-book manuscript called *Janie Bell*, which concerned a white nurse's adoption of a black baby found abandoned in a city street. She then submitted it to Doubleday, a respected New York firm. At first, Doubleday responded enthusiastically to Tarry with the offer of a contract; then, under pressure from company's southern retail accounts, the publisher backtracked, deciding instead to issue the book under the firm's less prestigious Garden City imprint. Tarry later found a happier publishing home at Viking, but her career remained a modest one, with the odds for greater success heavily stacked against her.

During the 1970s, however, the new forward momentum generated in the previous decade continued to build and, with more than a dozen books to his credit as an illustrator, Jerry Pinkney increasingly found himself near the center of the action. The publication of *Zeely* in 1967 had introduced Virginia Hamilton as a powerful new African American voice in the realm of children's fiction. Four years later, Pinkney's selection to create the cover for Hamilton's much anticipated second novel, *The Planet of Junior Brown*, put the artist in the spotlight, especially after Hamilton's book won a 1972 Newbery Honor. Another plum assignment—the illustrations for the Council on Interracial Books for Children fiction award winner for 1974—linked Pinkney's work for the first time with that of another writer with whom he was to have a long-standing professional

On a Black Oak a Few Yards Away Was a Huge White X, 1975, Illustration for *Song of the Trees*

relationship, Mildred D. Taylor. The Dial Press published Taylor's *Song of the Trees* the following year. From then onward, Dial's editor, Phyllis Fogelman, played a pivotal role in both collaborators' careers, as she did in the careers of several other important African American authors and artists including Julius Lester, Tom Feelings, and Valerie Flournoy.

The establishment of the Coretta Scott King Awards for children's literature (for writing from 1970 and for illustration as well since 1974) added further momentum. With its clarion call for African American cultural pride, so too did Alex Haley's *Roots*—which became a phenomenon both as an international bestseller (1976) and television miniseries (1977). Valerie Flournoy's *The Patchwork Quilt*, with Pinkney's illustrations (1985), presented young children with a multigenerational story that touched on some of the same core themes that made Haley's work so compelling.

While *The Snowy Day*, *Stevie*, and *The Patchwork Quilt* were staking out the territory for a new tradition of picture books about contemporary and historical African American themes, interest in folklore was also intensifying within the children's-book community. Bruno Bettelheim in his widely heralded *The Uses of Enchantment* (1976) argued forcefully for the developmental value for young people of exposure to traditional tales. The psychoanalyst's endorsement had the effect of galvanizing demand for authentic renderings of stories from many cultures. Pinkney became closely associated with this trend both through a three-volume collaboration with Julius Lester aimed at revivifying the Brer Rabbit tales for a new generation, and through a number of picture-book retellings of the tales of Aesop, Hans Christian Andersen, and others.

Having grown up with the Aesop and Andersen stories at home, Pinkney viewed the opportunity to illustrate them later in life as a chance to reconnect with his storytelling roots on an intimate level. His work in this vein also served to burnish his reputation as an artist of scope. Bookstores during the 1980s and afterward tended to shelve picture books on African American themes, if they carried them at all, as a special interest category rather than with "mainstream" picture books like *Where the Wild Things Are* and *Make Way for Ducklings*. Pinkney was determined not be pigeonholed. The awarding of the 2010 Caldecott Medal for *The Lion and the Mouse*, a not quite wordless interpretation of one of Aesop's best known fables, suggested that he had indeed managed to escape that fate.

The Lion and the Mouse seems early on to have had the special significance of a crossroad work, a project for gathering up some of the many strands of a long, productive career: Pinkney's

affection for the classic Western stories of his childhood, his fascination with the animal world and the medium of watercolor, and his felt connection with the life and landscapes of Africa, whose Serengeti Plain serves in his version as the story's setting. As such, *The Lion and the Mouse* was a fitting enough book for which finally to win the medal after five Caldecott Honors and countless other professional accolades over more than forty years. The medal came at a time when the next generation of African American artists and writers for children (including former students of Pinkney's and several members of his own family) had established flourishing careers of their own, and when the publishing community (despite financial uncertainties that had once again brought to the fore that industry's most conservative instincts) continued to maintain some commitment to putting the work of such artists and writers into children's hands. One decade into the new millennium, it was still too soon to claim that the dream of a racially inclusive American children's literature had been fully realized. But the distance traveled down that road during Jerry Pinkney's professional lifetime has been nothing short of extraordinary, and few artists could be said to have worked half as hard to lead the way as he.

JERRY PINKNEY:
American Illustrator

Gerald L. Early, Ph.D.

"**AFRICAN** Americans survived in a way that actually made a contribution." — *Jerry Pinkney*

"Publishers sought out black artists to illustrate black subject matter and the work of black writers [in the late 1960s and early 1970s]," African American illustrator Jerry Pinkney writes in explaining how his career was launched. "And there I was—it was almost like a setup." Pinkney's way of saying that he was in the right place at the right time begs the question of how did the time of Pinkney's rise as an illustrator become the right time.

Liberal white educator and author Nancy Larrick's article, "The All-White World of Children's Books" appeared in the September 11, 1965 issue of the *Saturday Review of Literature* and created something of a firestorm in the children's book publishing world. It argued that very few children's books depicted African American characters, the few that did so were usually unflattering, even derogatory portraits, that publishers were afraid of publishing more diverse or ethnically rich children's literature for fear of often white, especially white southern patrons and bookstore owners, and finally that most children's books, in the matter of dealing with race, were not only detrimental to the hearts and minds of black children but to white children as well. The article appeared just a few months after President Lyndon Johnson gave the Commencement address at Howard University entitled "To Fulfill These Rights," a reference to the title of President Truman's Civil Rights Commission report in 1947 called "To Secure These Rights." Johnson made one of the most fervent commitments ever by an American president to complete civil rights for African Americans including political and economic parity with whites. In August, Congress passed the Voting Rights Act, just one year after passing the Civil Rights Act, the major legislation that black civil rights leaders had been pursuing for decades. Over the course of the ensuing decades, these legislative acts changed profoundly racial attitudes and racial ideology in the United States. Alas, all was not sweetness, light, and racial progress, when, between August 11 and 15, 1965, the black section of Los Angeles, Watts, exploded with four days of violent rioting that killed thirty-four people. During the rest of the 1960s, this type of mass racial violence would scar much of urban America. Also, 1965 was the same year that the Council on Interracial Book for Children was founded, dedicated not only to integrating the content of children's books but securing more African American writers and illustrators to create books for children. Their efforts led to the discovery of such famous African American children's writers as Virginia Hamilton, Walter Dean

Untitled (Woman with Hoe), 2004, Selma to Montgomery National Heritage Trail, National Park Service, Alabama

Minty Told her Mother and Father What Happened, 1996, Illustration for *Minty: A Story of a Young Harriet Tubman*

Myers, and Mildred Taylor as well as opened publishing doors to illustrators like Tom Feelings and a young Jerry Pinkney, only twenty six years old in 1965 and still making his way as a professional commercial artist.

But black writers and illustrators did not emerge simply because whites, for political, cultural or economic reasons, now sought them. The Black Power Movement, which came roaring in, with its militant swagger and provocation, after 1965, when integration seemed to have encountered a dead end, and was especially exciting to younger African Americans, brought with it a preoccupation with the arts and with the psychological restoration of black identity. "Black is Beautiful" became the new slogan as many black Americans stopped straightening their hair and adopted African styles of dress. The Black Arts Movement, led by writers Amiri Baraka and Larry Neal and political activist Maulani Ron Karenga, produced poets, playwrights, musicians and visual artists, even political philosophers who espoused a black value system—the Kawaida—from which would come the African American holiday Kwanzaa. Black Americans were in search of black aesthetic, a way of seeing the world and themselves that was free of the oppressor's gaze. The main purpose of this Black Arts thrust was for black artists to produce works for blacks that would inspire them politically and knit them together culturally. Famous artists such as poet Nikki Giovanni and singer/songwriter Gil Scott-Heron, a forefather of Rap, emerged from this era. All of this, from President Johnson's push for civil rights to Baraka's cry for a revolutionary black art that completely eschewed and even opposed Eurocentric values, created the moment from which Jerry Pinkney, in his young manhood, emerged as a significant American illustrator, seeking jobs and opportunities, as any entrepreneur or self-employed artist must, as well as a mission and a purpose, as any artist should. He was part of a tide that radically transformed American culture, even popular American taste, through its challenge of the prevailing white hegemonic consensus. Every black artist coming of professional age during these years was a rebel whether or not he or she was consciously aware of it.

Jerry Pinkney, as a children's book illustrator, is also part of a tradition or at least part of an *aspiration* toward a tradition, of African Americans creating an anti-racist children's literature. In 1920, W. E. B. Du Bois, editor of the NAACP's house organ, the *Crisis,* along with black novelist Jessie Fauset, launched the first black children's magazine in the Black Atlantic World, *The Brownies' Book.* It lasted only two years but what propelled it into existence remains an important motivation

for many black creative artists: the need to counteract racist depictions of blacks in children's literature (Martha Finley's *Elsie Dinsmore* books are an obvious example) and to counteract racist illustrations of blacks, particularly of black children ("pickaninies" were a common advertising icon and used as images for sheet music, especially coon songs, and stereotyped images of Topsy and Little Black Sambo were among the most famous visual representations of blacks in the world by the early 20th century). But to counteract racist depiction in this realm requires something like the creation of an intricate black mythology of just so stories, fairy tales, legends, folk tales, tall tales, and story rhymes. In this regard, Pinkney's most important books are *Sam and the Tigers* (a recasting of Helen Bannerman's 1899 controversy classic, *The Story of Little Black Sambo*), *John Henry* (a recasting of the famous American folk tale about the black railroad worker who tried to beat a machine), *Uncle Remus: The Complete Tales* (recasting the famous stories of Joel Chandler Harris and illustrator A. B. Frost), all done with writer Julius Lester. Taken together, these books seem conceived "to right the wrongs of the original," to borrow Pinkney's words from his introduction to *Sam and the Tigers*, to reclaim and reshape a black presence and tradition in children's literature that includes *both* writing and illustration. This being the case, it should hardly come as a surprise that the historical period that most interests Pinkney, as he explained in an interview, is "slavery, plantation life." This period remains the aspect of the African American past most in need of reclamation and reshaping, most in need of the mythmaking power of the illustrator. It should also come as no surprise that Charles White, the great African American mural artist of the Depression (who did the landmark work, *Contribution of the Negro to American Democracy*, located at Hampton University), was a

Brer Rabbit and the Mosquitoes, 1987, Illustration for *The Tales of Uncle Remus*

Again, She Lit Another, 1999, Illustration for *The Little Match Girl*

particular source of inspiration for what he wanted his art to accomplish in transforming not just American art but American history and black people's place in it. Finally, in this way, Pinkney's mission differs little from that of Lois Mailou Jones, the most prominently featured illustrator in *The Brownies' Book* in depicting black children and black mythological characters in a way that fully humanizes them while making them a source of wonderment to the magazine's child readers.

Jerry Pinkney was born in 1939 in Philadelphia, Pennsylvania, a city where, at that time, ethnic blocks existed cheek-by-jowl against one another in a cauldron of mixing and ethnic isolation. It was hard as an African American not to grow up in that city without feeling a sense of being apart, of otherness, but equally impossible to grow up without knowing people who were unlike yourself. Pinkney seems to have absorbed this contradictory social training into his work. He has drawn more than just African Americans. Indeed, he has drawn all sorts of people, plants, and animals in his work. "Only probably fifty percent of my work deals with my own culture. The other works really celebrate other cultures as well." Among other children's books he has illustrated have been versions of Hans Christian Andersen's *The Ugly Duckling, The Little Match Girl,* and *The Nightingale* as well as Rudyard Kipling's *Rikki-Tikki-Tavi*. His work has appeared in venues other than children's books. He designed the first nine stamps in the U. S. Postal Service's black heritage series. His work was featured on the cover of *National Geographic*, a considerable feat as that magazine now almost exclusively features photography.

He has of course received all the rewards and honors that an illustrator of his talent and longevity has the right to expect, including the Caldecott Medal for his 2009 adaptation of the Aesop fable, *The Lion and the Mouse*. At this point in his career, he stands as the dean of African American illustrators, a sort of school and conceptual originator unto himself, not unlike Howard Pyle, in the sense of having created such an unmistakable and influential approach to the illustration as a pure narrative device that can evoke a time within a cosmic sense of timelessness. His work, as much as that of any other major illustrator, has come to define the post-World War II American century.

The Lion, 2009, Cover illustration for *The Lion & The Mouse*

DRAW WHAT YOU KNOW

Steven Heller

"**WRITE** what you know," the standard creative writing workshop mantra, applies just as much to illustrators as to writers these days. In this age of merging media it is essential for artists to 'draw what you know'—and what you'd like to know, and what you'd like others to know too. Don't keep it pent up. Everyone likes a good story. And every illustrator has a good story to tell—personal or otherwise. Sometimes these tales are conveyed through pictures alone, other times through word and image. And if the illustrator cannot write (since many become visual artists because they cannot or, more to the point, are afraid to write), then that is why a higher power created collaborators and editors.

Let's turn back the clock. Once upon a time, illustrators were primarily illuminators of authors' texts (they weren't slaves per se, but they were nevertheless indentured to the word). Cartoonists, however, were considered independent thinkers who translated thoughts into word and image. Cartoonists made statements; illustrators mimicked or interpreted. Although the constraint did not stop them from exhibiting a visual personality, nonetheless they often lacked a literary voice. Fast forward to today: These traditional boundaries have long since blurred, and today drawing is, well, *writing* with pictures—a verbal-visual language that speaks to young and old with much the same complexity as text-alone narratives.

Children's books and comics have long been the primary venues for the marriage of these talents. In fact, with rare exceptions, children's books were the sole outlet. Now, with the inception in the 1980s of the publishing genre of graphic novels, illustrators (and cartoonists and comics artists and, for that matter, painters and photographers) have found another means to convey stories, the themes of which have exponentially expanded to include very complex material, not the least including illustrative autobiography, memoir and a hybrid of the two. Writing and drawing 'what you know' is practiced more vociferously than ever—revealing more intimate revelations.

Autobiographical works are variously conceived for different effects. Some are transcriptions from distinct memories of the past and present. Others probe into hazy or mysterious historical pasts. These demand in-depth research that often uncovers incredible secrets. *Maus* by Art Spiegelman, for example, the comic that arguably launched the graphic novel genre, was a labor

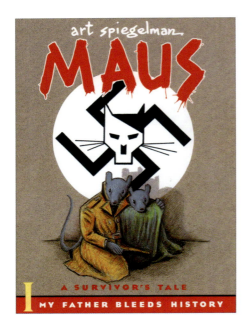 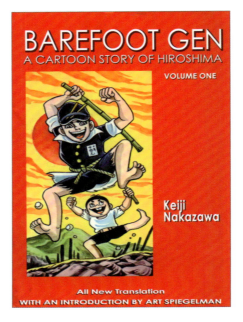

of emotional discovery. The protagonists, Spiegelman's parents depicted as mice, victims of Nazi (cats) persecution and ultimately survivors of the Holocaust, are presented in this form only after intense exploration. The anthropomorphic conceit was a means for Spiegelman to both attach and detach from the pain that he lived through as a child of survivors (In fact, his mother had committed suicide when he was in college and his father—the primary source—grieved until his death). Yet after years of relentless interrogation, a narrative emerged that formally combined the language of comics and children's books, and was as historically accurate as possible.

The Holocaust, which was once a taboo subject for children's books, was initially considered a callous—even tasteless—theme for comic books. But when presented as autobiography through the voices of those who endured it, critical resistance to the book evaporated. Before *Maus*, *Barefoot Gen*, a Japanese manga by Keiji Nakazawa, about a six year old boy who survives the atomic blast in Hiroshima, tackled equally difficult material combining first-person narrative with historical documentation. As the first Japanese manga to be translated in the United States, it doubtless inspired the wave of autobiography and memoir to follow. Children's books have

left: Cover image of *Maus: A Survivor's Tale* by Art Spiegelman.
right: Cover image of *Barefoot Gen: A Cartoon Story of Hiroshima*, Vol. I by Keiji Nakazawa.

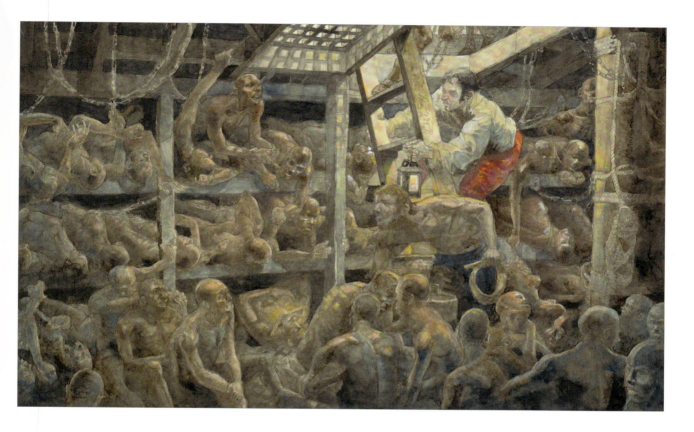

circuitously benefited from the increased thematic range of graphic novels, if not as memoir per se, as stories drawn from real life that was heretofore taboo.

I don't actually recall reading any comic or children's books drawn from intimate autobiography when I grew up in the 1950s in New York City. Most of my books were fairy tales and benign animal stories with banal images. Other than those ubiquitous *Classics Illustrated*s, comic book adaptations of classic novels—and some of these, like *Three Years Before the Mast*, were fictional memoirs—children's literature tread lightly if at all in this area. It is possible that such things existed, but either veiled behind layers of symbolism and allegory or kept away from my impressionable self. Of course, there were various biographies that were the official, myth-perpetuating hagiographies of famous people, but these do not count. Editorial attitudes began

In the Slave Hold, 2005, Illustration for *The Old African*

changing in the late 1960s, along with so much other turmoil in American society, when a new generation that gradually pushed the boundaries of appropriateness. Children's book author/illustrators took chances and entered an inner realm that was the precursor of the 'draw what you know—and what you'd like to know' philosophy.

Jerry Pinkney appears to have adopted this concept early in his career. Although the majority of his books are not autobiographical in the conventional sense, the fact that he was African American entering in a white dominated field—a field that ostensibly ignored the African American experience except as stereotyped folklore—provided an autobiographical imperative. "I wanted to show that an African American artist could make it in this country on a national level in the graphic arts," he once said. "I want to be a strong role model for my family and for other African Americans." Not only that, he sought to bring the classic tales of African Americans to the fore as integral components of the larger American culture. His author collaborators, notably Julius Lester, had the same mission. And Pinkney's impressionistic representational illustrations for the likes of *John Henry* and *The Last Tales of Uncle Remus* (both by Lester) helped raise the perception of these folkways away from those Disney caricatures that fostered dubious racial archetypes.

Of all the myraid stories Pinkney has illustrated, *Back Home* and *The Sunday Outing* by Gloria Jean Pinkney (his wife), suggest the most autobiographical resonance. Whether these are composites or direct recollections does not matter, the portrait, particularly in the latter book, of young Ernestine and her great-aunt Odessa, is a window to a distinctly loving family life that paints a alternative picture to the contemporary urban black myths and attitudes of today. Pinkney captures the warmth of the family and the essence of the moment in time. And this can only be rooted in 'draw what you know.'

The Old African, 2005, Cover Illustration for *The Old African*

And Mis Poinsettia Gave Mirandy Two of Her See Through Scarves, 1988, Illustration for *Mirandy and Brother Wind*

In the Parlor Listening to the Sunday Gospel Hour, 1994, Illustration for *Sunday Outing*

WATERCOLOR INTO WOOD

Joyce K. Schiller, Ph.D.

THERE is nothing more wonderful than opening a children's book and feeling pulled-in by its images. Jerry Pinkney's watercolor illustrations draw a reader into the story and have a fixed hold in the mind's eye.

Pinkney's focus on training as a graphic artist and an illustrator stemmed in part from his youthful challenge with reading due to dyslexia. His love of and innate talent for drawing gave the young artist a place where he could excel, and in his teens, he studied commercial art at one of Philadelphia's specialty high schools, Dobbins Vocational School. From there he moved on to the Philadelphia College of Art (now known as the University of the Arts) as a scholarship student majoring in design.

Early assignments, like a series of commissioned designs for *RCA* record album covers, brought into alignment the worlds of graphics and illustration. Inspiration for imagery most often came from within the music, allowing him to work conceptually and symbolically through the careful arrangement of representational elements.

Many of Pinkney's early story illustration commissions are drawings in black and white with cross-hatched lines indicating a plethora of tones and details, as in his images for the 1972 publication, *JD*, the Mari Evans story of an African American boy growing up in a housing project in a small mid-western city. An imaginative child, the book's protagonist conjures up the image of a friendly dog with tongue wagging, who wants JD to play with him. To illustrate this bit of whimsy, Pinkney rendered the boy in sure crisp lines, with the boy's shoes and sox the darkest aspect of this black and white picture, helping to ground the image in reality. A fantasy, the romping dog that attempts to lure JD into playing with him is drawn with more delicate pencil lines that emerge from behind the figure. Even though the fluffy creature pictured is all in JD's mind, Pinkney portrays him convincingly, from the black of the dog's nose leather to his shining dark eyes peering out from fluffy fur. Other details, like the dog's oversize paws, tell the viewer that, like JD, this imaginary friend still has some growing up to do. Because of his nuanced use of light and dark, Pinkney's black and white images relay a world of colorful information to the reader.

Black and white drawings also accompany Virginia Hamilton's 1980 story *Jahdu*, the third in a series of tales about this trickster character. In free-verse we learn that Jahdu is able to shake his magical dust over things, causing them to sleep or wake up. Dancing in the breeze as it awakens

Gustav Mahler, c. 1965, Album cover illustration for RCA Records

nature, Jahdu's dust is cleverly expressed as it drifts through the air. Stolen by his shadow, Jahdu's magic is later regained, and in the book's finale, Jahdu is wrapped in its shimmer, which unwinds as he runs through the night. All that is visible of Jahdu in this final illustration are his hands and feet poking out from this cosmic magic as he moves along a star-stream. In this drawing, Pinkney laid down black ink in random patterns over his initial pencil, mimicking the appearance of a night sky punctuated by the shimmer of star-shine. The artist merges the magical with an approximation of the real, creating believable images of the fantastical.

In the late 1970s, Jerry Pinkney shifted his attention from illustrating fiction to the exploration of history. His first historical commissions came from the United States Postal Service, for which he created a series of Black Heritage stamps celebrating African American achievement. For a 1984 *National Geographic* article on the Underground Railroad Pinkney's watercolor image of escaped slaves crossing a bridge to freedom was used as the cover for the July issue of the magazine. While the pencil and inked framework for the illustration clearly shows through the watercolor painting, it is the strong colors and distinct expressions on the figure's faces that convey a sense of determination, wonder, fear, and joy, bound into the story of the escape. Bundled against the cold in patched, inadequate clothing, Pinkney helps us see the dignity and resolve necessary to make such a journey.

Since his earliest graphic work, Pinkney has always embraced the use of color for its ability to convey mood and emotion. In his 1988 illustrations for Patricia C. McKissack's book, *Mirandy and Brother Wind*, the artist does not shy away from illustrating the invisible. For McKissack's story, and perhaps inspired by the extended cheeks of the Zephyr in Botticelli's *Birth of Venus* (1485), Pinkney envisions Brother Wind as an elegantly attired dandy in shades of blue, wearing a top hat and cape over his high collared shirt, waistcoat, overcoat, and checked slacks. Like the image of Jahdu's dust dancing in the air, Brother Wind flits through the story's pages flattening

JD and the Imaginary Dog, 1972, Illustration for *JD*

Jahdu Shimmered on a Star-Stream, 1980, Illustration for *Jahdu*

the grasses in the meadow and terrorizing the hens in Ma Dear's hen house. The artist's ability to convincingly portray folded and draped fabric—especially the checks of Mirandy's dress and the multi-patterned fabrics of Mis Poinsettia skirt—conveys a sense of volume and movement while establishing a stimulating visual foundation.

I have long been a fan of artist designed wall papers, so it was wonderful to realize that Pinkney has created wall paper patterns, finishes, and textures for some of the stories he has illustrated. For his 1990 *Home Place* by Crescent Dragonwagon, Pinkney's period wall papers were published as endpapers and on the title page of the book. An older oak branch and acorn-patterned paper is revealed beneath the new flowered design in his illustration, reminiscent of a home in which the only tangible things that remain are the foundation and a half-standing chimney. If you look carefully in his interior scenes, those same papers on the walls of the long-gone house are seen.

For the 2003 publication of *God Bless the Child*, based on the song by Billie Holiday and Arthur Herzog, Jr., endpapers were again inspired by wallpaper designs. In the beginning of the story, the essence of the family's rural wooden home is revealed in the book's front endpaper, which lovingly recreates its horizontal wooden boards with their grain and age stains. Pinkney's mastery of watercolor technique is visible in his marriage of charcoal and watercolor to render the rough planks of wood. At the end of the story, when the family settles in a northern city reminiscent of Chicago, the wall covering representing the more affluent northern city with its vertical stripes interspersed with leaf rings surrounding blooming gardenias. Pinkney chose gardenias as a visual reference to Billie Holiday, who wrote the words to the song, since they were her signature flower.

Since the late 1980s, Jerry Pinkney has worked with author Julius Lester in the production of four books that reimagine the *Tales of Uncle Remus*, first adapted and compiled by Joel Chandler Harris. The artist's skill at producing realistic images of animals is without equal, but just as fabulous is his ability to convincingly clothe anthropomorphic animal and human characters, so that images of the two interacting seem plausible. as in *Brer Rabbit and Miss Nancy* from *The Last Tales of Uncle Remus*. Not only does the body of Brer Rabbit conform to nature, but the clothing Pinkney imagines for this well-loved trickster also conforms to a rabbit's reality. In the image, our attention is focused on the interaction between the two characters, but we also enjoy the richness of the

Gardenia-patterned Wall Paper, 2003, Illustration for *God Bless the Child*

scene, with colorful laundry drying on the clothesline, vegetables gathered in baskets on the porch, sunflowers smiling in the yard, and a farmer ploughing a field in the distance.

In the late 1990s, Pinkney began to produce illustrations for a variety of books inspired by biblical stories. The first, *David's Songs: His Psalms and Their Story* was selected and edited by Colin Eisler. The artist's illustrations lovingly enhance the story of this great and conflicted man. In the parting of the Red Sea, Pinkney displays his mastery of the watercolor medium. An image of a body of water created in watercolor may be thought to be an easy translation, but his art reveals just how controlled and layered the application of paint must be to render it "swirled in fear" as Moses and Aaron led the children of Israel "through great waters." Imagining the wet spray that spewed from foamy waves, Pinkney dotted a scrim of white gouache over the fleeing masses. In 2002, Pinkney again focused on images of vast waters in his book, *Noah's Ark*. For his painting of the end of the deluge and the great wind that helped to clear the waters away, Pinkney illustrates a progression of time as the grey and rainy skies move off to the upper right and the winds begin to blow, stirring the waters. In *After Forty Days and Forty Nights the Rain Stopped Falling*, the cloud filled sky and the waters below echo one another in their hues and composition, with white gouache spray foaming up from the cresting wave.

Pinkney's convincing ability to convey translucency is demonstrated in *The Hired Hand: An African-American Folktale* retold by Robert D. San Souci in 1997. Well-honed drawings establish a basis for Pinkney's illustrations, and if one looks carefully at his watercolors, pencil lines that serve as the foundation for the finished piece are clearly observed. In the case of *Saw Dust Do What You Must*, the drawn lines for the figure of the old man being encased in sawdust are evident, and one can almost smell the freshly shaved wood, portrayed in thinly applied, transparent layers of color. It is interesting to note the order in which Pinkney works as he creates his watercolor images. First, he draws the illustration on the paper and when complete he covers the paper with a watercolor wash in either warm or cool tones, depending on the way he intends the finished illustration to look. Then, he stretches the paper over his work board and applies watercolor and gouache, layer by layer until the image is compete.

For Julius Lester's 2005 publication of *The Old African* we are fortunate to be able to see not only a variety of finished watercolor illustrations for this book, but also some of the working drawings that Pinkney produced in the process. Several cover concepts are evident, as poses and

Brer Rabbit and Miss Nancy, 1994, Illustration for *Last Tales of Uncle Remus*

Opening of the Red Sea, 1992, Illustration for *David's Songs: His Psalms and Their Story*

Noah Had Faith in God, 2002, Illustration for *Noah's Ark*
Following page: *Saw Dust Do What You Must*, 1997, Illustration for *The Hired Hand*

scenarios are varied in pencil and brown ink, with corrections and changes recorded in black. The finished version is a further modification of a circled study sketch featuring an African man in the water, looking out at an imaginary field of slave ships. Most of the versions for this cover merge the real with the imagined. The artist's studies and finished work reveals the exacting process used to construct this and other striking images.

For the retelling of the tale of *Little Red Riding Hood*, Pinkney chose to place the story in winter-time to make it distinctive among the many published versions of the story. By so doing, he was able to create lusciously detailed snow-filled winter landscapes within a context he established. My personal favorite merges the outdoors with a view inside grandmother's cottage. Wonderfully subtle, the action of the story is rendered as a shadow on the wall, as the woodsman kills the wolf with his ax, thereby saving her from harm. Equally illuminating is his painting of the wolf dressed in the grandmother's nightgown and cap, tucked up tightly in her bed. On the wall overlooking the bed is a picture of grandmother with her hand to her mouth in surprise at finding that the wolf is actually pretending to be *her*.

Pinkney's 2010 Randolph Caldecott Medal winning book, *The Lion & the Mouse*, reveals his talent for creating believable portrayals of animals, and through their expressions, making them communicate directly with readers. When the once-fierce Lion is captured in a rope net, we feel the weight and stature of the great creature as it is flipped and cradled within its trap. The expressive rendering of the lion's eyes and roaring mouth convey his distress, and the wild array of layered colors in the lion's mane convey its mass and texture.

Pinkney's 2009 series of illustrations for a book about the International *Sweethearts of Rhythm*, an accomplished 1940s sixteen-piece all-girl swing band, convey the "color and texture of the band's vibrant music." Pinkney melded watercolor and collage elements to create his experimental

Cover Concept, 2005, Illustration for *The Old African*

Little Red Riding Hood Met a Sly Wolf, 2007, Illustration for *Little Red Riding Hood*
Following page: *Lion's Capture*, 2009. Illustration for *The Lion & The Mouse*

Take the 'A' Train, 2009 Illustration for *Sweethearts of Rhythm*

images, as in *Take the 'A' Train*, where he conveyed the beat of the music's syncopated quarter notes through the inclusion of torn pieces of sheet music and song titles that circle a swing-dancing couple.

Jerry Pinkney is a detailed observer of people, places, and things. His true talent is the ability to translate those observations into illustrations so amazing that when we first turn the page we are drawn to the wonder of what we see. Later, when we return to our favorite picture books, as though visiting old friends, we are more likely to notice the myriad of exquisite details that make up these pictures. For example, the way Pinkney indicates the wandering mists of fragrance by smudged misty lines wandering through the landscape in the story "The Fragrance of Paradise" in *Journeys with Elijah*; the details of yellowing grasses in the Serengeti with a line of ants marching along one blade as the mouse moves over a bump in the grassy landscape unaware that it is the lion's tail in *The Lion and The Mouse*; and the way wood looks when freshly sawn as opposed to its darkened surface as it ages, and the scent and mist of it when pictured in the form of sawdust as seen in images for *The Hired Hand*. How wonderful it is that Jerry Pinkney is able to turn watercolor into wood.

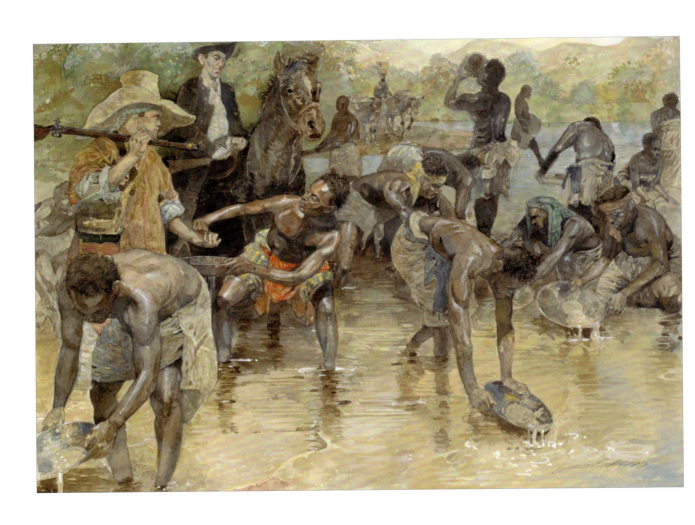

Africans at the Water Washing, 1992, Illustration for *"The Cruelest Commerce: African Slave Trade"* for *National Geographic*, © National Geographic Society. All rights reserved.

Catalogue Contributors

Dr. Gerald L. Early is Merle Kling Professor of Modern Letters, Professor of English and of African and Afro-American Studies, Director of the Center for Humanities, and a Fellow of the American Academy of Arts and Sciences at Washington University in St. Louis. He is the editor of several volumes, including *This Is Where I Came In: Black America in the 1960s*, *The Sammy Davis, Jr., Reader*; *The Muhammad Ali Reader*; *Body Language: Writers on Sport*; *Speech and Power*; *Lure and Loathing: Essays on Race, Identity, and the Ambivalence of Assimilation*; and *My Soul's High Song: The Collected Works of Countee Cullen*. Professor Early is the author of *The Culture of Bruising: Essays on Prizefighting, Literature, and Modern American Culture*, which won the 1994 National Book Critics Circle Award for criticism. Other works are *One Nation Under a Groove: Motown and American Culture*; *Daughters: On Family and Fatherhood*; and *Tuxedo Junction*. The recipient of a Whiting Writer's Award and a General Electric Foundation Award, he also consulted on Ken Burns' documentary films, *Baseball*, *Jazz*, and *The War*, and is a regular commentator on National Public Radio's *Fresh Air*.

Steven Heller is an award-winning art director and the author, co-author, or editor of more than one hundred books on design, illustration, and popular culture. A journalist, critic, and commentator, he has written for many publications, including *Print*, *U&lc*, *I.D. Magazine*, *Affiche*, *Graphis*, *Creation*, *Eye*, *Design*, *How*, *Oxymoron*, *Design Issues*, *Mother Jones*, *Speak*, *Graphis*, and the *New York Times Book Review*. He worked as art director of *The New York Times* for thirty-three years, and has been editor of the *AIGA Journal of Graphic Design*, a forum for design writing and criticism, since its inception in the early 1980s. The co-chair and founder of the MFA Designer as Author Program at the School of Visual Arts in New York, he is also Special Consultant to the President of SVA for New Programs, and writes the "Visuals" column for the *New York Times Book Review*. *Illustration: A Visual History*, *Graphic Wit: The Art of Humor in Design*, *Iron Fists: Branding the 20th Century Totalitarian State*, and *Pop: How Graphic Design Shapes Popular Culture* are among his many insightful publications.

Leonard S. Marcus is a noted children's book historian, author, and critic who has written many acclaimed books about literature for young people and the authors and artists who create it, including *Funny Business*; *Golden Legacy: How Golden Books Won Children's Hearts, Changed Publishing Forever, and Became an American Icon Along the Way*; *Minders of Make-Believe*; *Margaret Wise Brown: Awakened by the Moon*; and many others. His incisive book reviews have appeared in every issue of *Parenting* magazine for twenty-one years, and his commentary is also published regularly in *The New York Times Book Review* and in *Sight Reading*, a column on illustrated books for *The Horn Book*. A three-time juror for *The New York Times* Best Illustrated Book of the Year prize, he has also curated exhibitions highlighting the art of picturebook illustration at the Eric Carle Museum of Picturebook Art, New York Public Library, New School for Social Research, Boston Athenaeum, Joslyn Art Museum, and Katonah Museum of Art.

Jerry Pinkney is an award-winning artist who began his creative journey in the field of illustration in 1960. A native of Philadelphia, he studied at the Philadelphia School of Art, began his career as a graphic designer, and has been illustrating children's books since 1964. Memorable and richly conceived, his artworks have appeared in more than one hundred books, and have garnered well-deserved acclaim. The recipient of a Caldecott Medal, five Caldecott Honor Medals, five Coretta Scott King Awards, and four Coretta Scott King Honor Awards, and has received many commendations for his outstanding body of work, including the Original Art's Lifetime Achievement Award from the Society of Illustrators, New York, in 2006. His books have been translated into eleven languages and published in fourteen different countries.

In addition to his work in children's books, Pinkney has created illustrations for a wide variety of clients, including the U.S. Postal Service, the National Park Service, and *National Geographic* magazine. He served on the U.S. Postal Services Citizens Stamp Advisory Committee from 1982 to 1992, and in 2003, he was appointed to the National Council on the Arts/NEA, a prestigious position held for six years. A gifted educator, he has mentored aspiring illustrators at Pratt Institute, the University of Delaware, and the State University of New York University at Buffalo, and his work is featured among the permanent collections of Library of Congress, New York Public Library, Delaware Art Museum, and the Brandywine River Art Museum. Pinkney also holds Honorary Doctor of Fine Arts degrees from the Art Institute of Boston at Lesley University and from the Pennsylvania College of Art and Design.

Stephanie Haboush Plunkett is the Deputy Director and Chief Curator of the Norman Rockwell Museum. The recipient of a Master of Fine Arts degree from the School of Visual Arts, Illustration as Visual Essay, she is the author of two American Library Association Notable children's books and the curator of many exhibitions exploring the art of Norman Rockwell and the field of illustration, including *Witness: The Art of Jerry Pinkney; William Steig: Love & Laughter; Ephemeral Beauty: Al Parker and the American Women's Magazine: 1940–1960; LitGraphic: The World of the Graphic Novel; Building Books: The Art of David Macaulay;* and *The Art of The New Yorker: Eighty Years in the Vanguard,* among others. She began her professional career in museum education, and has previously held positions at the Brooklyn Museum, the Brooklyn Children's Museum, and the Heckscher Museum of Art.

Dr. Joyce K. Schiller is the Curator of the Rockwell Center for American Visual Studies at the Norman Rockwell Museum, the nation's first art history research institute devoted to the advancement of scholarship relating to the art of illustration. Previously, she served as Curator of American and Illustration Art at the Delaware Art Museum; Curator of American Art at Reynolda House Museum of American Art; and Senior Lecturer at the Saint Louis Art Museum. She earned her Ph. D. from Washington University in St. Louis in American art history, where her dissertation focused on the collaborative work of the sculptor of Augustus Saint-Gaudens and the architect Stanford White. *Witness: The Art of Jerry Pinkney, Illustrating Her World: Ellen B.T. Pyle*, and *Seeing the City: Sloan's New York* are among the many exhibitions that she has curated.

WITNESS: The Art of Jerry Pinkney   Exhibition Checklist

Designer to Illustrator

Untitled (Marionette)   1967
Illustration for *This Is Music*
(Boston: Allyn & Bacon, 1967)
Watercolor on paper
Collection of the Artist

Untitled (Angel)   1967
Illustration for *This Is Music*
(Boston: Allyn & Bacon, 1967)
Watercolor on paper
Collection of the Artist

Gustav Mahler   c. 1965
Album cover illustration for RCA Records
Watercolor and ink on paper
Collection of the Artist

Jazz Greats (Coleman Hawkins)   1984
Unpublished institutional calendar
   illustration for Smirnoff
Watercolor on paper
Collection of the Artist

Jazz Greats (Jelly Roll Morton)   1984
Unpublished institutional calendar
   illustration for Smirnoff
Watercolor on paper
Collection of the Artist

Jazz Greats (Roy Eldridge)   1984
Unpublished institutional calendar
   illustration for Smirnoff
Watercolor on paper
Collection of the Artist

Jazz Greats (Kid Ory)   1984
Unpublished institutional calendar
   illustration for Smirnoff
Watercolor on paper
Collection of the Artist

Steal Away   1971
Jacket illustration for *Steal Away: Stories
   of the Runaway Slaves*, by Abraham
   Chapman (New York: Praeger Publishers,
   1971)
Watercolor and pencil on paper
Collection of the Artist

Slave Hunters   1990
Jacket illustration for *The Underground
   Man*, by Milton Meltzer (Harcourt Brace
   Jovanovich, 1990)
Watercolor and pencil on paper
Collection of the Artist

Sarny   1997
Jacket illustration for *Sarny: A Life
   Remembered*, by Gary Paulsen (NY:
   Bantam Dell Publishing Group, 1997)
Watercolor and pencil on paper
Collection of the Artist

Family Traditions

Lumber Mill   1979
Illustration for *Childtimes: A Three-Generation
   Memoir*, by Eloise Greenfield and Lessie
   Jones Little (New York: Crowell, 1979)
Pencil on paper
Collection of the Artist

At the Train Station   1979
Illustration for *Childtimes: A Three Generation
   Memoir*, by Eloise Greenfield and Lessie
   Jones Little (New York: Crowell, 1979)
Pencil on paper
Collection of the Artist

In the Park   1979
Illustration for *Childtimes: A Three Generation
   Memoir*, by Eloise Greenfield and Lessie
   Jones Little (New York: Crowell, 1979)
Pencil on paper
Collection of the Artist

Vignette of Brother's Blue Corduroy   1985
Illustration for *A Patchwork Quilt*, by Valerie
   Flournoy (New York: Dial Books, 1985)
Watercolor and pencil on paper
Collection of the Artist

Tanya Snipped and Trimmed the Scraps   1985
Illustration for *A Patchwork Quilt*, by Valerie
   Flournoy (New York: Dial Books, 1985)
Watercolor and pencil on paper
Collection of the Artist

Tanya Always Found Time   1985
Illustration for *A Patchwork Quilt*, by Valerie
   Flournoy (New York: Dial Books, 1985)
Watercolor and pencil on paper
Collection of the Artist

Reds, Greens, Blues and Golds   1985
Illustration for *A Patchwork Quilt*, by Valerie
   Flournoy (New York: Dial Books, 1985)
Watercolor and pencil on paper
Collection of the Artist

Uncle Ferd   1990
Illustration for *Home Place*, by Crescent
   Dragonwagon (New York: Macmillan,
   1990)
Watercolor and pencil on paper
Collection of the Artist

In a Quiet Green Place 1990
Illustration for *Home Place*, by Crescent
  Dragonwagon (New York: Macmillan,
  1990)
Watercolor and pencil on paper
Collection of the Artist

Untitled (Wood Wall) 2003
Endpaper illustration for *God Bless the Child*,
  by Billie Holiday and Arthur Herzog, Jr.
  (New York: Harper Collins, 2003)
Watercolor and pencil on paper
Collection of the Artist

Untitled (Old and New Wallpaper) 1990
Endpaper illustration for *Home Place*, by
  Crescent Dragonwagon (New York:
  Macmillan, 1990)
Watercolor and pencil on paper
Collection of the Artist

Untitled (New Wallpaper) 1990
Title page illustration for *Home Place*, by
  Crescent Dragonwagon (New York:
  Macmillan, 1990)
Watercolor and pencil on paper
Collection of the Artist

Untitled (Wallpaper) 2003
Endpaper illustration for *God Bless the Child*,
  by Billie Holiday and Arthur Herzog, Jr.
  (New York: Harper Collins, 2003)
Watercolor and pencil on paper
Collection of the Artist

Untitled (Room Interior) 2003
Illustration for *God Bless the Child*, by Billie
  Holiday and Arthur Herzog, Jr. (New York:
  Harper Collins, 2003)
Watercolor and pencil on paper
Collection of the Artist

*In the Parlor Listening to the Sunday Gospel
Hour* 1994
Illustration for *Sunday Outing*, by Gloria Jean
  Pinkney (New York: Dial Books, 1994)
Watercolor and pencil on paper
Collection of the Artist

This Is My Wedding Satchel 1994
Illustration for *Sunday Outing*, by Gloria Jean
  Pinkney (New York: Dial Books, 1994)
Watercolor and pencil on paper
Collection of the Artist

Waiting at the Station for the Train 1994
Illustration for *Sunday Outing*, by
  Gloria Jean Pinkney (New York: Dial
  Books, 1994)
Watercolor and pencil on paper
Collection of the Artist

A Welcoming Hug 1995
Illustration for *Tanya's Reunion*, by Valerie
  Flournoy (New York: Dial Books, 1995)
Watercolor and pencil on paper
Collection of the Artist

Tanya Stopped at the Room 1995
Illustration for *Tanya's Reunion*, by Valerie
  Flournoy (New York: Dial Books, 1995)
Watercolor and pencil on paper
Collection of the Artist

Classic Tales

Scrooge and Ghost c.1968
Illustration for *A Christmas Carol*, by Charles
  Dickens (Boston: Allyn & Bacon)
Watercolor on paper
Collection of the Artist

Gulliver with Little Girl Giant 1977
Illustration for *Gulliver's Travels*, by Jonathan
  Swift (Philadelphia: Franklin Library, 1977)
Pencil on paper
Collection of the Artist

Gulliver Whispering into Man's Ear 1977
Illustration for *Gulliver's Travels* by Jonathan
  Swift (Philadelphia: Franklin Library, 1977)
Pencil on paper
Collection of the Artist

Victory 1979
Illustration for "Victory" in *These Thirteen*,
  by William Faulkner (Philadelphia: The
  Franklin Library, 1979)
Pencil on paper
Collection of the Artist

A Justice 1979
Illustration for "A Justice" in *These Thirteen*,
  by William Faulkner (Philadelphia: The
  Franklin Library, 1979)
Pencil on paper
Collection of the Artist

Mistral 1979
Illustration for "Mistral" in *These Thirteen*,
  by William Faulkner (Philadelphia: The
  Franklin Library, 1979)
Pencil on paper
Collection of the Artist

John Henry 1994
Cover illustration for *John Henry*, by Julius
  Lester (New York: Dial Books, 1994)
Watercolor and pencil on paper
Collection of the Artist

When John Henry Was Born 1994
Illustration for *John Henry*, by Julius Lester
  (New York: Dial Books, 1994)
Watercolor and pencil on paper
Collection of the Artist

Let's Have a Contest 1994

Illustration for *John Henry*, by Julius Lester (New York: Dial Books, 1994)
Watercolor and pencil on paper
Collection of the Artist

Home and Garden in India 1997
Title page illustration for *Rikki-Tikki-Tavi*, by Rudyard Kipling (New York: Morrow, 1997)
Watercolor and pencil on paper
Collection of the Artist

Rikki-tikki Came to Breakfast 1997
Illustration for *Rikki-Tikki-Tavi*, by Rudyard Kipling (New York: Morrow, 1997)
Watercolor and pencil on paper
Collection of the Artist

In the Melon Bed 1997
Illustration for *Rikki-Tikki-Tavi*, by Rudyard Kipling (New York: Morrow, 1997)
Watercolor and pencil on paper
Collection of the Artist

The Poor Little Girl Walked Along the Icy Streets 1999
Illustration for *The Little Match Girl*, by Hans Christian Andersen (New York: Phyllis Fogelman Books, 1999)
Watercolor and pencil on paper
Collection of the Artist

So the Poor Little Girl Went On With Nothing 1999
Illustration for *The Little Match Girl*, by Hans Christian Andersen (New York: Phyllis Fogelman Books, 1999)
Watercolor and pencil on paper
Collection of the Artist

Her Little Hands and Feet Were Almost Stiff with Cold 1999
Illustration for *The Little Match Girl*, by Hans Christian Andersen (New York: Phyllis Fogelman Books, 1999)
Watercolor and pencil on paper
Collection of the Artist

Again, She Lit Another 1999
Illustration for *The Little Match Girl*, by Hans Christian Andersen (New York: Phyllis Fogelman Books, 1999)
Watercolor and pencil on paper
Collection of the Artist

Scrooge and Ghost, c.1968, Illustration for *A Christmas Carol*

Brer Rabbit 1999
Cover (spine) illustration for *Uncle Remus: The Complete Tales*, retold by Julius Lester (New York: Phyllis Fogelman Books, 1999)
Watercolor and pencil on paper
Collection of the Artist

Brer Rabbit and Uncle Remus 1999
Fronticepiece illustration for *Uncle Remus: The Complete Tales*, retold by Julius Lester (New York: Phyllis Fogelman Books, 1999)
Pencil on paper
Collection of Mimi Kaden

Brer Rabbit Goes Back to Mr. Man's Garden 1987
Illustration for *The Tales of Uncle Remus* retold by Julius Lester (New York: Dial Books; Bodley Head, 1987)
Watercolor and pencil on paper
Collection of the Artist

Brer Rabbit and the Mosquitoes 1987
Illustration for *The Tales of Uncle Remus* retold by Julius Lester (New York: Dial Books; Bodley Head, 1987)
Pencil on paper
Collection of the Artist

How Brer Rabbit Became a Scary Monster 1987
Illustration for *The Tales of Uncle Remus* retold by Julius Lester (New York: Dial Books; Bodley Head, 1987)
Pencil on paper
Collection of the Artist

Brer Rabbit Scares Everybody 1988
Illustration for *More Tales of Uncle Remus* retold by Julius Lester (New York: Dial Books, 1988)
Pencil on paper
Collection of the Artist

Rikki-Tikki Comes To Breakfast, 1997, Illustration for *Rikki-Tikki-Tavi*,

The Race 1988
Illustration for *More Tales of Uncle Remus* retold by Julius Lester (New York: Dial Books, 1988)
Pencil on paper
Collection of the Artist

Taily-po 1990
Illustration for *Further Tales of Uncle Remus* retold by Julius Lester (New York: Dial Books, 1990)
Pencil on paper
Collection of the Artist

Brer Deer and King Sun's Daughter 1990
Illustration for *Further Tales of Uncle Remus* retold by Julius Lester (New York: Dial Books, 1990)
Watercolor and pencil on paper
Collection of the Artist

Brer Deer and King Sun's Daughter 1990
Illustration for *Further Tales of Uncle Remus* retold by Julius Lester (New York: Dial Books, 1990)
Pencil on paper
Collection of the Artist

Brer Rabbit and Miss Nancy 1994
Illustration for *Last Tales of Uncle Remus* retold by Julius Lester (New York: Dial Books, 1994)
Watercolor and pencil on paper
Collection of the Artist

Why Guinea Fowl Are Speckled 1994
Illustration for *Last Tales of Uncle Remus* retold by Julius Lester (New York: Dial Books, 1994)
Watercolor and pencil on paper
Collection of the Artist

The Adventures of Simon and Susanna 1994
Illustration for *Last Tales of Uncle Remus* retold by Julius Lester (New York: Dial Books, 1994)
Pencil on paper
Collection of the Artist

Little Red Riding Hood Met a Sly Wolf 2007
Illustration for *Little Red Riding Hood*, by Charles Perrault (New York: Little, Brown and Company/Hachette Book Group, 2007)
Watercolor and pencil on paper
Collection of the Artist

Settled into the Bed to Wait for His Next Meal 2007
Illustration for *Little Red Riding Hood*, by Charles Perrault (New York: Little, Brown and Company/Hachette Book Group, 2007)
Watercolor and pencil on paper
Collection of the Artist

What Great Eyes You Have! 2007
Illustration for *Little Red Riding Hood*, by Charles Perrault (New York: Little, Brown and Company/Hachette Book Group, 2007)
Watercolor and pencil on paper
Collection of the Artist

With One Stroke of His Ax 2007
Illustration for *Little Red Riding Hood*, by Charles Perrault (New York: Little, Brown and Company/Hachette Book Group, 2007)
Watercolor and pencil on paper
Collection of the Artist

Mouse in Lion's Paw Print 2009
Illustration for *The Lion & The Mouse,* by Aesop (New York: Little, Brown and Company/Hachette Book Group, 2009)
Watercolor and pencil on paper
Collection of the Artist

Mouse and Lion's Tail 2009
Illustration for *The Lion & The Mouse,* by Aesop (New York: Little, Brown and Company/Hachette Book Group, 2009)
Watercolor and pencil on paper
Collection of the Artist

Grrrr (Lion Picks Up Mouse) 2009
Illustration for *The Lion & The Mouse,* by Aesop (New York: Little, Brown and Company/Hachette Book Group, 2009)
Watercolor and pencil on paper
Collection of the Artist

Lion's Capture 2009
Illustration for *The Lion & The Mouse,* by Aesop (New York: Little, Brown and Company/Hachette Book Group, 2009)
Watercolor and pencil on paper
Collection of the Artist

Lion, Mouse, and Net 2009
Illustration for *The Lion & The Mouse,* by Aesop (New York: Little, Brown and Company/Hachette Book Group, 2009)
Watercolor and pencil on paper
Collection of the Artist

Three Little Kittens 2010
Book jacket illustration for *Three Little Kittens*, (New York: Dial Books, 2010)
Watercolor and pencil on paper
Collection of the Artist

They Spun and Leaped 2010
Illustration for *Three Little Kittens*, (New York: Dial Books, 2010)
Watercolor and pencil on paper
Collection of the Artist

Jahdu Dust Waking Flowers, 1980, Illustration for *Jahdu*

You Silly Kittens 2010
Illustration for *Three Little Kittens*, (New York: Dial Books, 2010)
Watercolor and pencil on paper
Collection of the Artist

Lost Your Mittens 2010
Illustration for *Three Little Kittens*, (New York: Dial Books, 2010)
Watercolor and pencil on paper
Collection of the Artist

You Silly Kittens 2010
Illustration for *Three Little Kittens*, (New York: Dial Books, 2010)
Watercolor and pencil on paper
Collection of the Artist

Reconsidering History

JD and the Imaginary Dog 1972
Illustration for *JD*, by Mari Evans (New York: Doubleday & Co., 1972)
Pencil on paper
Collection of the Artist

JD and the 817 Stone 1972
Illustration for *JD*, by Mari Evans (New York: Doubleday & Co., 1972)
Pencil on paper
Collection of the Artist

JD Opened His Eyes 1972
Illustration for *JD*, by Mari Evans (New York: Doubleday & Co., 1972)
Pencil on paper
Collection of the Artist

I Jumped Out of the Feathery Bed as Big Ma Climbed from the Other Side. 1975
Illustration for *Song of the Trees*, by Mildred D. Taylor (New York: Dial Books, 1975)
Pencil on paper
Collection of the Artist

On a Black Oak a Few Yards Away Was a

Huge White X   1975
Illustration for *Song of the Trees,* by Mildred
   D. Taylor (New York: Dial Books, 1975)
Pencil on paper
Collection of the Artist

Mr. Andersen Stared at Mama.   1975
Illustration for *Song of the Trees,* by Mildred
   D. Taylor (New York: Dial Books, 1975)
Pencil on paper
Collection of the Artist

On the Ground Lay Countless Trees   1975
Illustration for *Song of the Trees* by Mildred
   D. Taylor (New York: Dial Books, 1975)
Pencil on paper
Collection of the Artist

Jahdu Dust Waking Flowers   1980
Illustration for *Jahdu*, by Virginia Hamilton
   (New York: Greenwillow, 1980)
Ink and pencil on paper
Collection of the Artist

Jahdu Lunged for His Shadow   1980
Illustration for *Jahdu*, by Virginia Hamilton
   (New York: Greenwillow, 1980)
Ink and pencil on paper
Collection of the Artist

The Night Was Black and Full   1980
Illustration for *Jahdu*, by Virginia Hamilton
   (New York: Greenwillow, 1980)
Ink and pencil on paper
Collection of the Artist

Jahdu Had A Round Ball Of Shimmer   1980
Illustration for *Jahdu*, by Virginia Hamilton
   (New York: Greenwillow, 1980)
Ink and pencil on paper
Collection of the Artist

You're My Shadow Attached to Me   1980
Illustration for *Jahdu*, by Virginia Hamilton
   (New York: Greenwillow, 1980)
Ink and pencil on paper
Collection of the Artist

Jahdu Shimmered on a Star-Stream   1980
Illustration for *Jahdu*, by Virginia Hamilton
   (New York: Greenwillow, 1980)
Ink and pencil on paper
Collection of the Artist

*Harriet Tubman Conducts Escaped Slaves
Into Canada*   1984
Cover illustration for "Escape from
   Slavery: Underground Railroad," *National
   Geographic* (July 1984)
Watercolor, pencil and ink on paper
Collection of the Artist

Thousands of People Sought to Aid Slaves
1984
Illustration for "Escape from Slavery:
   Underground Railroad," *National
   Geographic* (July 1984)
Watercolor, pencil and ink on paper
Collection of the Artist

*And Mis Poinsettia Gave Mirandy Two of Her
See-Through Scarves*   1988
Illustration for *Mirandy and Brother Wind*, by
   Patricia C. McKissack (New York: Knopf,
   1988)
Watercolor and pencil on paper
Collection of the Artist

*Ridge Folk Talked 'bout How Mirandy and
Ezel Had Won the Junior Cake Walk*   1988
Illustration for *Mirandy and Brother Wind*, by
   Patricia C. McKissack (New York: Knopf,
   1988)
Watercolor and pencil on paper
Collection of the Artist

Untitled (Africans At the Water Washing)
1992
Illustration for "The Cruelest Commerce:
   The African Slave Trade from Ghana to
   Brazil," *National Geographic* (1992)
Watercolor and pencil on paper
Collection of the Artist

Untitled (Africans in Their Village)   1992
Illustration for "The Cruelest Commerce:
   The African Slave Trade from Ghana to
   Brazil," *National Geographic* (1992)
Watercolor and pencil on paper
Collection of the Artist

Untitled (Rough Treatment)   1992
Illustration for "The Cruelest Commerce:
   The African Slave Trade from Ghana to
   Brazil," *National Geographic* (1992)
Watercolor and pencil on paper
Collection of the Artist

Through The Snow   2004
Illustration for "Farce at The Winter Palace:
   The Russian Revolution" *Reader's Digest*
Watercolor and pencil on paper
Collection of the Artist

Helping Father From Bed   2004
Illustration for "Farce at The Winter Palace:
   The Russian Revolution" *Reader's Digest*
Watercolor and pencil on paper
Collection of the Artist

Distributing Food   2004
Illustration for "Farce at The Winter Palace:
   The Russian Revolution" *Reader's Digest*
Watercolor and pencil on paper
Collection of the Artist

Cooking Over an Open Fire 1994
Illustration for Booker T. Washington
 National Monument, Rocky Mount,
 Virginia, 1994
Watercolor and pencil on paper
Collection of the Artist

*Gather Tobacco Leaves and Readying Them
for Drying* 1994
Illustration for Booker T. Washington
 National Monument, Rocky Mount,
 Virginia, 1994
Watercolor and pencil on paper
Collection of the Artist

*Minty Told Her Mother and Father What
Happened* 1996
Illustration for *Minty: A Story of a Young
 Harriet Tubman*, by Alan Schroeder (New
 York: Dial Books, 1996)
Watercolor and pencil on paper
Collection of the Artist

There's Something I Want to Show You 1996
Illustration for *Minty: A Story of a Young
 Harriet Tubman*, by Alan Schroeder (New
 York: Dial Books, 1996)
Watercolor and pencil on paper
Collection of the Artist

Old Ben Taught Her How to Swim 1996
Illustration for *Minty: A Story of a Young
 Harriet Tubman*, by Alan Schroeder (New
 York: Dial Books, 1996)
Watercolor and pencil on paper
Collection of the Artist

Minty Began to Cry 1996
Illustration for *Minty: A Story of a Young
 Harriet Tubman*, by Alan Schroeder (New
 York: Dial Books, 1996)
Watercolor and pencil on paper
Collection of the Artist

Escape at Night 1996
Cover illustration for *The Underground
 Railroad Handbook*, National Park Service,
 1997
Watercolor and pencil on paper
Collection of the Artist

The Saw Mill 1997
Title page illustration for *The Hired Hand*,
 by Robert D. San Souci (New York: Dial
 Books, 1997)
Watercolor and pencil on paper
Collection of the Artist

The Water Wheel 1997
Illustration for *The Hired Hand*, by
 Robert D. San Souci (New York: Dial
 Books, 1997)
Watercolor and pencil on paper
Collection of the Artist

Saw Dust Do What You Must 1997
Illustration for *The Hired Hand*, by
 Robert D. San Souci (New York: Dial
 Books, 1997)
Watercolor and pencil on paper
Collection of the Artist

*Sam Sawed the Wooden Shape Into Four
Pieces* 1997
Illustration for *The Hired Hand*, by
 Robert D. San Souci (New York: Dial
 Books, 1997)
Watercolor and pencil on paper
Collection of the Artist

In the Courtroom 1997
Illustration for *The Hired Hand*, by
 Robert D. San Souci (New York: Dial
 Books, 1997)
Watercolor and pencil on paper
Collection of the Artist

The Hoof prints of Mustangs 1998
Illustration for *Black Cowboy, Wild Horses*, by
 Julius Lester (New York: Dial Books, 1998)
Watercolor and pencil on paper
Collection of the Artist

Then the Rain Came 1998
Illustration for *Black Cowboy, Wild Horses*, by
 Julius Lester (New York: Dial Books, 1998)
Watercolor and pencil on paper
Collection of the Artist

They Thought He Was a Horse 1998
Illustration for *Black Cowboy, Wild Horses*, by
 Julius Lester (New York: Dial Books, 1998)
Watercolor and pencil on paper
Collection of the Artist

When the Herd Set Out 1998
Illustration for *Black Cowboy, Wild Horses*, by
 Julius Lester (New York: Dial Books, 1998)
Watercolor and pencil on paper
Collection of the Artist

Yes, the Strong Gets More 2003
Illustration for *God Bless the Child*, by Billie
 Holiday and Arthur Herzog, Jr. (New York:
 Harper Collins, 2003)
Watercolor and pencil on paper
Collection of the Artist

Old Home 2003
Illustration for *God Bless the Child*, by Billie
 Holiday and Arthur Herzog, Jr. (New York:
 Harper Collins, 2003)
Watercolor and pencil on paper
Collection of the Artist

Modern City 2003
Illustration for *God Bless the Child*, by Billie
 Holiday and Arthur Herzog, Jr. (New York:
 Harper Collins, 2003)
Watercolor and pencil on paper
Collection of the Artist

Money, You Got Lots O' Friends 2003

Illustration for *God Bless the Child*, by Billie Holiday and Arthur Herzog, Jr. (New York: Harper Collins, 2003)
Watercolor and pencil on paper
Collection of the Artist

Untitled (Man on Crate)   2004
Illustration for *Plural Response*, Selma to Montgomery National Historic Trail, National Park Service, Alabama
Watercolor and pencil on paper
Collection of the Artist

Untitled (Woman with Hoe)   2004
Illustration for *Plural Response*, Selma to Montgomery National Historic Trail, National Park Service, Alabama
Watercolor and pencil on paper
Collection of the Artist

Untitled (Man with Folded Arms)   2004
Illustration for *Plural Response*, Selma to Montgomery National Historic Trail, National Park Service, Alabama
Watercolor and pencil on paper
Collection of the Artist

Untitled (Woman with Fan)   2004
Illustration for *Plural Response*, Selma to Montgomery National Historic Trail, National Park Service, Alabama
Watercolor and pencil on paper
Collection of the Artist

The Old African   2005
Illustration for *The Old African*, by Julius Lester (New York: Dial Books, 2005)
Watercolor and pencil on paper
Collection of the Artist

In the Slave Hold   2005
Illustration for *The Old African*, by Julius Lester (New York: Dial Books, 2005)
Watercolor and pencil on paper
Collection of the Artist

At the Beach   2005
Illustration for *The Old African*, by Julius Lester (New York: Dial Books, 2005)
Watercolor and pencil on paper
Collection of the Artist

As If There Were Steps to Walk On   2005
Illustration for *The Old African*, by Julius Lester (New York: Dial Books, 2005)
Watercolor and pencil on paper
Collection of the Artist

Welcome Home!   2005
Illustration for *The Old African*, by Julius Lester (New York: Dial Books, 2005)
Watercolor and pencil on paper
Collection of the Artist

Preparatory Drawings   2005
Studies for *The Old African*, by Julius Lester (New York: Dial Books, 2005)
Ink on paper
Collection of the Artist

Book Dummies   2005
Illustration for *The Old African*, by Julius Lester (New York: Dial Books, 2005)
Pencil and Ink on paper
Collection of the Artist

Cover Concepts   2005
Illustration for *The Old African*, by Julius Lester (New York: Dial Books, 2005)
Ink on paper
Collection of the Artist

Lee's Resignation 1861   2007
Brochure illustration for Arlington House, The Robert E. Lee Memorial, Virginia, 2007, National Park Service
Watercolor and pencil on paper
Collection of the Artist

Freedman's Village, ca 1864   2007
Brochure illustration for Arlington House, The Robert E. Lee Memorial, Virginia, 2007, National Park Service
Watercolor and pencil on paper
Collection of the Artist

Amelia   2008
Illustration for African Burial Ground Interpretive Center, New York, 2008
Watercolor and pencil on paper
Collection of the Artist

Mary   2008
Illustration for African Burial Ground Interpretive Center, New York, 2008
Watercolor and pencil on paper
Collection of the Artist

Peter Williams, Sr.   2008
Illustration for African Burial Ground Interpretive Center, New York, 2008
Watercolor and pencil on paper
Collection of the Artist

Cuffee   2008
Illustration for African Burial Ground Interpretive Center, New York, 2008
Watercolor and pencil on paper
Collection of the Artist

The Sweethearts of Rhythm   2009
Illustration for *Sweethearts of Rhythm*, by Marilyn Nelson (New York: Dial Books, 2009)
Mixed media on paper
Collection of the Artist

Cotton Club, 2009, Illustration for *Sweethearts of Rhythm*

Cotton Club   2009
Illustration for *Sweethearts of Rhythm*, by
   Marilyn Nelson (New York: Dial Books,
   2009)
Mixed media on paper
Collection of the Artist

Take the "A" Train   2009
Illustration for *Sweethearts of Rhythm*, by
   Marilyn Nelson (New York: Dial Books,
   2009)
Mixed media on paper
Collection of the Artist

Lady, Be Good   2009
Illustration for *Sweethearts of Rhythm*, by
   Marilyn Nelson (New York: Dial Books,
   2009)
Mixed media on paper
Collection of the Artist

Water Fountairs   2009
Illustration for *Sweethearts of Rhythm*, by
   Marilyn Nelson (New York: Dial Books,
   2009)
Mixed media on paper
Collection of the Artist

That Man of Mine   2009
Illustration for *Sweethearts of Rhythm*, by
   Marilyn Nelson (New York: Dial Books,
   2009)
Mixed media on paper
Collection of the Artist

Finale   2009
Illustration for *Sweethearts of Rhythm*, by
   Marilyn Nelson (New York: Dial Books,
   2009)
Mixed media on paper
Collection of the Artist

Biblical Tales

Opening of the Red Sea   1992
Illustration for *David's Songs: His Psalms
   and Their Story*, edited and introduced by
   Colin Eisler (New York: Dial, Books, 1992)
Watercolor and pencil on paper
Collection of the Artist

The Lion of Judah   1992
Illustration for *David's Songs: His Psalms
   and Their Story*, edited and introduced by
   Colin Eisler (New York: Dial, Books, 1992)
Watercolor and pencil on paper
Collection of the Artist

The Owl and Jerusalem   1992
Illustration for *David's Songs: His Psalms
   and Their Story*, edited and introduced by
   Colin Eisler (New York: Dial, Books, 1992)
Watercolor and pencil on paper
Collection of the Artist

Journeys with Elijah   1999
Cover illustration for *Journeys with Elijah:
   Eight Tales of the Prophet*, by Barbara
   Diamond Goldin (New York: Gulliver
   Books, Harcourt, Brace & Co., 1999)
Watercolor and pencil on paper
Collection of the Artist

Seven Good Years   1999
Illustration for *Journeys with Elijah: Eight
   Tales of the Prophet*, by Barbara Diamond
   Goldin (New York: Gulliver Books,
   Harcourt, Brace & Co., 1999)
Watercolor and pencil on paper
Collection of the Artist

The Fragrance of Paradise   1999
Illustration for *Journeys with Elijah: Eight
   Tales of the Prophet*, by Barbara Diamond
   Goldin (New York: Gulliver Books,
   Harcourt, Brace & Co., 1999)
Watercolor and pencil on paper
Collection of the Artist

Noah Did as the Lord Commanded   2002
Illustration for *Noah's Ark*, (New York:
   SeaStar Books, 2002
Watercolor and pencil on paper
Collection of the Artist

God Remembered Noah and His Family
2002
Illustration for *Noah's Ark*, (New York:
   SeaStar Books, 2002)
Watercolor and pencil on paper
Collection of the Artist

*After Forty Days and Forty Nights the Rain
Stopped Falling*   2002
Illustration for *Noah's Ark*, (New York:
   SeaStar Books, 2002)
Watercolor and pencil on paper
Collection of the Artist

Noah Had Faith in God   2002
Illustration for *Noah's Ark*, (New York:
   SeaStar Books, 2002)
Watercolor and pencil on paper
Collection of the Artist

Witness: The Art of Jerry Pinkney
is a Norman Rockwell Museum Publication.

Norman Rockwell Museum Exhibition Dates: November 13, 2010 through May 30, 2011

This exhibition catalogue is made possible, in part, with generous support from The Max and Victoria Dreyfuss Foundation, Penguin Group, Inc. and Little, Brown Books for Young Readers, a division of The Hachette Group.

Compilation copyright © 2010 by Norman Rockwell Museum.
All images are reproduced with the permission of the copyright holder, Jerry Pinkney, except as otherwise noted. All rights reserved. No part of this publication may be reproduced in any form without written permission from the publisher.

Distributed in 2010 by Norman Rockwell Museum
PO Box 308, 9 Glendale Road, Stockbridge, Massachusetts 01262
www.nrm.org

ISBN: 978-0-9615273-5-8

Front cover: *John Henry* by Jerry Pinkney, 1994. Illustration for *John Henry*, by Julius Lester.
Back cover: *Mary* by Jerry Pinkney, 2008. Illustration for African Burial Ground Interpretive Center, New York.
Title page: *Her Little Hands and Feet Were Almost Stiff With Cold* by Jerry Pinkney, 1999. Illustration for *The Little Match Girl*, by Hans Christian Andersen.
Page 4: *The Fragrance of Paradise*, 1999, Illustration for *Journeys with Elijah: Eight Tales of The Prophet*

Designed by Rita Marshall.
Edited by Wren Bernstein, Stephanie Haboush Plunkett, and Joyce K. Schiller.
Production by Rita Marshall, Mindy Belter, Stephanie Haboush Plunkett, and Joyce K. Schiller.
Printed by Qualprint, Pittsfield, Massachusetts.
First Edition 2010
Second Edition 2013

Additional Credits
Page 36: Title page image of *The Snowy Day* by Ezra Jack Keats. Used by permission of Viking Children's Books, A division of Penguin Young Readers Group. All rights reserved.
Page 37: Cover image of *Stevie* by John Steptoe. Copyright © 1969 by John I Steptoe. Harper & Row, Publishers, New York, Evanston, and London.
Page 54: Cover image of *Maus: A Survivor's Tale* by Art Spiegelman. Copyright © 1973, 1980, 1981, 1982, 1983, 1984, 1985, 1986 by Art Spiegelman. Pantheon Books, a division of Random House, Inc., Publisher, New York.
Page 54: Cover image of *Barefoot Gen: A Cartoon Story of Hiroshima, Vol. I* by Keiji Nakazawa. Copyright © 2004 by Keiji Nakazawa. First serialized in the manga anthology, *Weekly Sho-nen Jump* in 1973. Published by Last Gasp of San Francisco, California.